With Hope in Our Hearts

PREVIOUS PUBLICATIONS

DAVID SHEPPARD

Built as a City
Bias to the Poor
Better Together

DEREK WORLOCK

Seek Ye First
Take One at Bedtime
English Bishops at the Council
Turn and Turn Again
Better Together
With Christ in the Wilderness
Bread Upon the Waters

With Hope in Our Hearts

David Sheppard and Derek Worlock

Hodder & Stoughton
LONDON SYDNEY AUCKLAND

To the people of Liverpool whose indomitable spirit has been
an imspiration to both of us

British Library Cataloguing in Publication Data
A record for this book is available from the British Library

ISBN 0 340 62133 8

Typeset by Hewer Text Composition Services, Edinburgh
Printed and bound in Great Britain

Hodder and Stoughton Ltd
A division of Hodder Headline PLC
338 Euston Road
London NW1 3BH

Contents

Note All quotations from Scripture are from the *New Revised Standard Version* unless otherwise shown

Introduction

When in 1988 we published *Better Together*, as an account of our Christian partnership in Liverpool, there was evident surprise at the range of our shared interests and activities. For many this was welcome, though for some it presented a problem, usually summed up as 'Church and politics'. One columnist from a prestigious Sunday newspaper told us of the difficulty experienced by the literary editor of his voluminous paper which had failed to review the book. A quick glance at the contents of *Better Together* had suggested that we had dealt with political issues as well as spiritual concerns, so the editor had not known whether to pass it to his political colleagues or to hand it over to the religious correspondent for review. 'You seem to have got the two themes mixed up,' the columnist told us. We tried in vain to explain that this was not a mistake. Because in practice today these two aspects of life and of our concern were so frequently intertwined, love of God and love of neighbour led us into considerations which she saw as Church and politics, but we recognised as our dual commitment 'to Christ and to our city'.

Our partnership in the fulfilment of that commitment arises initially and in large measure from our mutual recognition of each other's baptism. We believe that we are both truly baptised into the life, death and resurrection of Christ. Now that much of the old language of controversy has been cast to one side, we recognise that we hold in common the central truths of the Christian faith, grounded in Holy Scripture and confessed in the Catholic creeds. We share in the mission entrusted to his followers by Christ, and the responsibility to try to lead others to the acceptance of Christ's Gospel. We believe that this Gospel must be lived out in the world, day after day, and not just restricted to worship in church buildings.

We believe strongly that our proclamation of that Gospel must help our hearers to appreciate the relevance of Christ's teaching to the real

1

problems of their lives today, at home and at work. Of course this is where the 'politics' aspect of the confusion is likely to develop. A good example of this would be our involvement in efforts to secure good housing, something quite basic to human dignity. How can we leave our neighbours, whom we are to love, roofless, homeless or deprived of decent housing? We see it as an inescapable part of our Christian commitment to them. But in the eyes of many others such concern is only a short distance away from political involvement.

In 1990 the Bible Reading Fellowship published our Lent Book, *With Christ in the Wilderness*. In this book also we produced a fully shared text and we were able to write more explicitly for the Christian family. This meant that we could begin with Gospel events and spiritual truths and then show how we believed that these led on to action and sometimes to taking sides in public affairs. We welcomed this opportunity. All too often, when we offer comment on public affairs, the media are unlikely to quote the Christian reasoning which leads us to particular conclusions. They simply want to know where we stand on issues of current interest.

It is claimed that there is a new generation every five years, each with its own particular interests. Certainly prevailing opinions, attitudes, fashions and priorities among young people can change in that time. The examples and incidents given in *Better Together*, written more than six years ago, while remaining historically true – snapshots to provide the contemporary background to our record – are inevitably already dated. As we have moved around the country since then, the request has increasingly been made to 'tell us what has happened recently'. If a week in politics is now proverbially a long time, six years in Merseyside have brought many changes, in home life, commerce and industry, even of Government ministers and local community leaders.

During the same period some new approaches have been attempted to heal longstanding wounds. While there have been some encouraging signs, often the wounds are still festering. In 1993 Merseyside was accorded Objective One status in the European Community, the only region in England to be so designated because of its measured poverty. On the other hand there has been talk of 'green shoots of hope' in the area. We have had what in some ways has been a unique opportunity to reflect on the various approaches and their results in personal and human terms. It is this reflection which has made us realise that this further book needs to be more than just an updating or a new edition of *Better Together*.

One result of the earlier book was a steady flow of invitations to the pair of us to do 'the double act' in widely different parts of Britain and Ireland, and on one occasion in South Africa. Far from agreeing with the gloomy prognostication that 'the steam has gone out of ecumenism', we have taken heart from the enthusiasm we have met on these visits. We have seen that enthusiasm translated into willingness to work at building up trust and practical collaboration in the mission of Christ. It has been most encouraging to find that others have been spurred on by our reflection on our partnership through what have been momentous years in Liverpool. If it can flourish against the background of sectarianism, once so bitter in our city, surely – it is argued – something similar can be developed elsewhere.

On the occasion of our making visits to interested areas elsewhere, we have almost invariably been questioned as to how our relationship and collaboration works out in practice. Often we have been asked whether a similar partnership might not be achieved more generally. We have found that not infrequently such a relationship already exists, at least in embryo if not fully developed. All that is required is more formal recognition and commitment. Significantly in most places this improved relationship and united action are desired by many more Churches and congregations than just our own.

In Merseyside, with MARCEA (Merseyside and Region Churches Ecumenical Assembly) there had already been established a triple Presidency, with the Anglican Bishop, the Roman Catholic Archbishop and one of the Free Church Leaders elected by the Free Church sector of MARCEA. Providence clearly took a hand and after the retirement of the URC Moderator, the Revd John Williamson, who had played so big a part in the setting up of MARCEA, the Revd Dr John Newton, the new Chairman of the Methodist District, was duly elected the third Joint President.

It was not long before invitations began to arrive from various parts of the country, inviting a visit from 'the Liverpool Three'. In one sense that has been the most significant development of all. It has enabled us to speak and sometimes to act in the name of all the mainline Christian Churches in Merseyside. There is an obvious convenience in such an arrangement, but it has also proved an answer to those who would say to the pair of us 'That's all very well for you, Anglicans and Romans, but where are the others?' At a more personal level we have greatly enjoyed the wisdom, good humour and wide experience of John Newton. In this book we have thought it right to ask his comment on certain matters and to have his evaluation of the situation here, as he has found it, and to which we are confident he has in these last years made a major contribution. It is our hope that these combined reflections on many years of shared ministry may be a resource for the new team of Merseyside Church leaders who will follow us in the next few years.

In our partnership of service and witness, we have never tried to dodge the awkward issues and teachings about which we are not in agreement. Some of these we will discuss in later pages. A sea-change is brought about in considering quite serious differences once both parties are sensitive about why the other holds views conflicting with his own. But simply because we have often found deep and precious common ground, we do not ignore the problems remaining between our Churches. There are still conscientiously held differences in certain beliefs, practices and disciplines. But generally we can speak in terms of reconciliation, even though not yet of the fullness of 'communion' to which we believe that Christ is calling us. These issues have to be faced and in all honesty. There have been times when our separation in eucharistic worship has been most painful. Yet 'fudging' differences solves nothing. If for the sake of sharing friendship we were to break the disciplines of our own denomination, we would run the danger merely of creating what would in effect be one more Church of our own.

We should not be disheartened. The present insoluble or at least unsolved problems do not mean that we should give up and claim that we can make no further headway. Building on the bond of baptism and on faith held in common, we can with true integrity work together for the extension of God's Kingdom in the world and give joint witness to our faith in the living Lord. When progress seems reduced to a snail's pace, it is worth looking back over the last thirty years to see how far our Churches and other Christians have been able to come. After all, it is not so very long since we would have been unable to recite the Lord's Prayer together at a Ministers' Fraternal.

We have witnessed astonishing developments in ecumenical relations and collaboration, and not just locally or on a personal level. Yet the importance of this local level work for Christian unity cannot be exaggerated. Academic achievements of top level theologians and Church leaders may point the way, but cannot effect Christian unity – regardless of the attitudes, relationships and beliefs of the communities they lead. Generals must not lose touch with their troops on the ground.

This realisation has been at the heart of recent initiatives whereby the British Council of Churches made way for the carefully-prepared 'instruments', set up after the Inter-Church Process, 'Not Strangers but Pilgrims', of the 1980s. In this process all three of us have been actively engaged, and it seems more than a coincidence that our *Better Together* slogan should be reflected in the new bodies: Churches Together in England (CTE); Action of Churches Together in Scotland (ACTS); CYTUN (which means 'together' in Welsh); and finally the Council of Churches for Britain and Ireland. It was argued that these titles were clumsy. We have answered that they describe just where we are at the present time: together and for the most part reconciled, but not yet fully one. What happens at local level has a real influence on the policy, practices and relationships between our Churches and communities at the national and international levels.

One of the significant words of the last five years has been 'subsidiarity'. It has had its importance in the approach to ecumenism as well as in the relationship between nations making up the European Community. While in the political field it has sometimes been reduced to 'minimal interference', Pope John Paul has stressed that 'a community of a higher order should not interfere in the internal life of a community of a lesser order, depriving the latter of its functions, but rather should support in case of need, and help to co-ordinate its activities with the activities of the rest of society, always with a view to the common good' (*Centesimus Annus*, n. 48). Applied to so-called ecumenical instruments, it has meant collaboration of member bodies at a higher level, seeking not to take over but to assist the endeavours of Church communities at a local level, without swamping them.

John Macquarrie said that it was of the nature of God to 'let be'. By this he did not mean a *laissez-faire* God standing back from our world. He meant that God actively creates the kind of conditions in which members of the whole body of Christ can develop the part of the world where they are placed. At the same time each local expression of the body of Christ needs to recognise that we are part of one universal Church, which reaches across human barriers, be they of nationalism, tribalism, race, class or gender: and 'always with a view to the common good', as the Pope has written, though this is not always easy to determine. While we have been trying to grapple with these issues in Church circles, politicians have been wrestling with this same principle of subsidiarity. Some have appealed to the additional concept of solidarity. But others have expressed their opposition to European unity by appealing to fears, seeming at times to be fuelled by 'Little Englander' anxieties. Such an attitude is very different from a proper insistence that appropriate decisions should be made in the appropriate place. The parallel with the ecumenical process has been remarkable.

The destructive harvest of religious intolerance leads us to affirm vigorously that tolerance ranks high in the hierarchy of virtues. Religious partisans seldom agree. They insist that loyalty and conviction must prove how their beliefs are the very truth and that all must be persuaded to submit to them in entirety. The tolerance which the ecumenical spirit proclaims is not some wishy-washy indifference, suggesting that all are climbing different sides of the same mountain. It is a tough tolerance, which holds to its loyalties with passion: among these is the conviction that God has gifted all human beings with free will and freedom of conscience to make informed decisions. This conviction ensures not only mutual regard, but loyal respect for all who sincerely name the name of Christ, and recognition of them as our brothers and sisters.

Our commitment to ecumenism has never been simply a matter of convenience or compromise, what we have called 'ecclesiastical joinery'. The urgency about Christian unity springs from our Lord's own prayer, the night before he died, 'that they may be one, that the world may believe'. Our divisions, conscientiously held, are still a stumbling-block to others. Our Churches, acknowledging their common task, have committed themselves to a Decade of Evangelism and/or Evangelisation. We do not feel that these words are so much an alternative as an indication that having 'named the name of Christ', we have the task of shedding the light of the Gospel throughout the world. In Merseyside and Lancashire there is little doubt that replacing the rivalry of old with increasing trust and visible partnership has in recent times won for the Church generally a great deal of street credibility. As we write about our own personal journey of faith, it is our hope that some will see the light of the Christian Gospel as good news in an often dark and changing world. We pray that the Decade may strengthen the confidence of believers, so that they may give a reason for the sometimes incoherent faith that is in them.

Once again we have tried to follow the same system of writing our book together. In fact, apart from personal reminiscence or argument (which, if used, we have carefully attributed and have placed in italic type), we have throughout jointly written the entire text. This is a slow process but means that we both own all that is written here. First, the detailed content of a chapter is discussed and agreed. Then one of us does a first draft, which is virtually rewritten by the other. There follows a succession of amendments and editing until at last there is total agreement of the whole text. This was the rather tedious but thorough method we used in writing *Better Together*, and we have repeated the process. It is true sharing and continues to deepen our understanding of each other's thoughts and hopes. One consequence is that in this book there are fewer personal insertions into the text. Six years after *Better Together*, we find that we share more, not less, and are often able to anticipate each other's thoughts and actions.

Once again we have enlisted the help of a group of friends who know us well and are able to advise as the text has emerged. Many of these are the same as last time: Grace Sheppard, Canon Eric James, Miss Pat Jones, Mrs Mary Tanner, and Bishop Vincent Nichols. We are no less grateful. To their number we have this time added Mgr James Dunne, Professor Noel Boaden, Mgr John Furnival and the Revd Tim Stratford. Of course we have also drawn in valuable contributions from our good friend, Dr John Newton. We have been wonderfully well supported by our households, especially by Grace Sheppard, Margaret Funnell and our two chaplains, who have inevitably had to bear additional burdens. Our thanks are due also to Mrs Jean Jones who has again undertaken the typing, and to Mr Tom Murphy who has helped with the photographs.

We believe that we have been greatly blessed and have had in these last years a unique experience of shared Christian ministry and witness.

Others have asked us to share the fruit of this experience with them. It is our hope that what follows truly contributes to the building up of this part of God's kingdom.

Liverpool, June 1994

1

The Pattern of Partnership

Our years together in Liverpool have produced a number of expressions to describe the relationship between the pair of us. The original description of the 'Double Act', which led in time to the more familiar 'Ecumenical Pantomime Horse' and 'Fish and Chips' (always together and seldom out of the newspaper), had to be adjusted more recently – at least on those occasions when we were joined by the Merseyside Free Church Moderator, Dr John Newton. It was in Exeter when we were first billed as 'the Liverpool Three', which some jokingly suggested placed us alongside 'the Guildford Four' and 'the Birmingham Six'. The important underlying fact is that people in Liverpool have come to expect the Churches to act together.

It was not always like that. Bitter sectarian divisions led at times to sectarian threats and violence from the bullyboys who sought to establish that Scotland Road was 'pure' Catholic, and that Netherfield Road up the hill in Everton was 'pure' Protestant. That was an example, with widespread consequences and even casualties, of the process now known as 'ethnic cleansing'. These bitter divisions did not simply turn on religious sectarian loyalties. As often happens, economic factors soon entered the scene and became intertwined with denominational differences. Behind many of these animosities there lay fears that the 'others' might turn up, take possession and take over 'our jobs'.

So great was the separation of adults and the segregation of children that in the past there was constant suspicion between the two communities. There would be sinister mutterings as well as shock if a 'mixed' marriage were announced. It is said that in one very respectable area there was scandal when the then Archbishop and Bishop were seen together exercising their dogs. In contrast, when more recently either of us has appeared at a public engagement without the other, the question has invariably been raised, 'Where's your friend today?' Even when, only a few years ago, we decided to take a short holiday together and, with Grace Sheppard and John Furnival (the archbishop's chaplain) to visit Assisi, the local barber, a Liverpool Catholic, needed some reassuring before admitting somewhat doubtfully, 'I suppose it's all right.' Suspicions, like loyalties, die hard.

We often try to explain that the important relationship between the two of us comes from our common baptism, and from our mutual recognition that we have both been drawn into the life and mission of Jesus Christ. That in itself would be sufficient reason for our co-operation in many matters. It arises from the Gospel which we share. The fact that we happen to be very good friends as well, sharing a whole range of interests, is something which we both regard as a bonus. That basic relationship of common purpose is something which we share with all the baptised. No matter what our role in the Church, we recognise our common dignity with all humankind. The particular message we bear to the world, and the service we must offer to all those in need is, of course, fired by our Gospel commitment. It is, if you like, the general context in which we love God and our neighbour.

Both of us are deeply involved in the engine-rooms of Bishops' Conference, House of Bishops, and national tasks of our own Churches. There have inevitably been moments when our knowledge and experience of each other's beliefs and practices have influenced our contribution to the debate. What has seemed a natural way of working for us has sometimes enabled us to bring an additional and valuable insight to the issue under consideration by our Churches.

We have had special circumstances in which to give witness to our Christian commitment and growing friendship. Our hope is that this has come to symbolise in some measure the shared commitment which today unites our Churches and the various Christian communities in Merseyside. This sharing is not all talk, but it is put to the test when applied to pooling resources of one kind or another, especially if it is a case of the 'haves' having to sustain the 'have-nots' when finance is required for some ecumenical project. In Merseyside that usually means that the Anglicans and the Roman Catholics customarily take one-third apiece, leaving the Free Churches to carry the remaining one-third. Often enough, this applies to the allocation of costs, but it is always somewhat easier when the resource to be shared happens to be something like media facilities or social services. At such a time the bonus of friendship and trust can assume a very important role.

In all this developing relationship, two other words have also assumed importance: covenant and partnership. In *Better Together* (chap. 5, 'Call to Partnership') we tried to set what had happened ecumenically here in Merseyside in the wider national context. At the historic meeting of Church representatives at Swanwick in September 1987, the leaders of all the Churches which had shared in the Inter-Church Process of prayer, reflection and debate on the nature and mission of the Church, reached a momentous breakthrough. In the Swanwick Declaration, issued at the end of the meeting, they attempted to describe how, under the guidance of the Holy Spirit, they had reached a common mind, and added: 'We now declare together our readiness to commit ourselves to each other under God. Our earnest desire is to become more fully, in His own time, the one Church of Christ, united in faith, communion, pastoral care and mission.' In the continuing pilgrimage in search of the fullness of unity, they recognised that there would not be the straitjacket of 'uniformity, but legitimate diversity'.

In the three years which followed, preparations were made and constitutions worked out for the four ecumenical instruments which have replaced the British Council of Churches. Today Churches Together in England and its sister bodies in Scotland and Wales are in full operation, along with the Council of Churches for Britain and Ireland. More important than developed paper organisation, new and happily improved relationships have been established, largely on the basis of lacing together initiatives of the Churches at local, regional and national levels, with decision-making left to the structure of the particular Church member. This excludes the danger of a super-Church issuing instructions to everyone else; it also leads to effective co-operation and partnership in mission. This is a sensitive area. It means now that at every level of the Churches' life important decisions must be taken by the normal decision-making bodies of each member-Church. The new ecumenical instruments are not distinct from the Churches: they are precisely Churches Together.

How has it worked out in practice, at national level as well as regionally? The process has not always been easy but already there are some real signs of progress, development and improved relationships. Learning to work out the basis of collaboration calls for perseverance and trust. This has been made no easier when the reorganisation called for has had to be carried through at a time when all Churches have been facing the financial stringency of recession. In some ways it seems to have proved easier to produce joint statements, shared policies and improved relationships than to share among member-Churches the services and responsibilities of particular agencies which were previously owned and conducted on a denominational basis. This has had to be faced, if costly duplication of effort and undesirable competition are to be avoided. On the other hand unwanted and ill-thought-out amalgamation of, say, relief agencies may serve merely to diminish effective activity and interest in established areas of concern. In practice it has sometimes been difficult to work out how an agency, previously staffed and financed by one Church, can produce services for many more member-Churches but on the same shoestring budget, especially when the demand is for cuts rather than expansion. This difficulty has still to be faced effectively when every Church is having to examine its budget. But it is not by comparative financial statements that these early evaluations and reviews are to be made.

At the national level, and in the four-nations Council of Churches for Britain and Ireland, the member-Churches recognise that there is an ecumenical dimension to all their life and work. As the Revd John Reardon, General Secretary of CCBI reported recently to the World Council of Churches, 'no longer is ecumenical engagement something that belongs only to the few. It is a recognised dimension of what it means to be a Christian.' The early years of the new structures have seen the deepening of the commitment of the Churches to one another. The Church leaders meet residentially twice a year to worship together, to study together, and to decide on what things the Churches can best do together. They try to reach their conclusions by consensus, but important decision-making requires consultation and reference back to member-Churches. In one sense this is slower, but the decision is owned and acted upon by all.

Public statements have been made by the four Presidents of Churches Together in England, who meet regularly and seem to have established good working practice. Matters of common concern, especially when the Christian view is needed in issues where there is public debate, have the expertise of several Churches to call on. Joint delegations to Government departments on a variety of matters have been brought together to good effect, often serviced and supported with research and advice provided either from Inter-Church House, where CTE and CCBI are based, or from the Anglican General Synod, the Methodist Central Hall or the Roman Catholic Bishops' Conference.

These early years of collaboration and sharing of resources as well as of objectives have inevitably brought some frustrations, not all of them yet resolved, but generally speaking, as David Sheppard reported in *The Church Times* after the 1994 Assembly of CCBI,

It was very clear that CCBI is not just a talking shop. This second assembly underlined for me the prime calling, above all denominational loyalties, to being a Christian. It stretched my Englishness by taking me into realities of Church life in Ireland, Scotland and Wales. It gave me glimpses of the Churches' networks engaging in a wide range of human needs and questionings. Sometimes I marvelled at how much is being achieved with very scarce resources. In a time when all the Churches are economising rather than expanding, I know how difficult it often is to find staff time in any of our Churches; and then additional time is demanded to work in partnership. But worshipping together with Christians from all our member Churches, I know that we must hang in there together: costly it may be, but this assembly has made it clear to me that working collaboratively we receive extra resources, wisdom and courage.

In making this short assessment of the progress of the ecumenical instruments established nationally in 1990, we are able also to draw on the experience of Church leaders in Merseyside in establishing our own regional organisation some years earlier. It was at Pentecost 1985 that, after much thought and consultation, Church communities here felt ready to commit themselves to one another in the common service of the Gospel. The detailed proposals for MARCEA had been carefully worked out, and the Church Leaders agreed to sign a covenant. This pledged their commitment to God and to one another in the pilgrimage and search for the visible unity of Christ's Church. The service to mark the signing of this act of covenant began in the Roman Catholic Cathedral and concluded in the Anglican Cathedral. A commemorative service, involving both cathedrals, has subsequently been held at Pentecost on alternate years, and includes the powerful symbolism of walking together along Hope Street, which links the two cathedrals.

It was a matter of great joy to all of us that in September 1990 it was decided that the ecumenical service to launch the Council of Churches for Britain and Ireland should be held in Liverpool. This followed the same form involving both Cathedrals, and the enormous crowd singing and walking along Hope Street. All the four nations' Church leaders were there to take part, led by Archbishop Runcie of Canterbury and Cardinal Hume of Westminster. The address was given by John Newton, one of the first Joint Presidents of Churches Together in England.

In the course of his sermon, entitled 'Pilgrims of Hope', John Newton said,

We meet in hope, and we meet in Liverpool. At one time to mention Liverpool and Christian unity in the same breath would have seemed a sick joke. This is a city like Glasgow and Belfast, which has been disfigured by bigotry and sectarianism. For years, Liverpool had a powerful Protestant party, segregated housing, and a firm belief that the orange and green could hardly belong to the same Christian rainbow. There are still a few contemporary ancestors, who haven't heard that peace has broken out, and are sadly bent on fighting the old wars. But the great majority of Christians on Merseyside have moved from rivalry to co-operation, and co-operation to commitment. Working and praying together, we have reached a degree of mutual understanding that has given us a common purpose. We are 'Churches Together', not yet fully one, but to a wonderful extent reconciled.

Sadly, a handful of 'contemporary ancestors' were waiting on the pavement outside to howl biblical abuse at the leaders of the Churches, as they made their way in procession from the Anglican Cathedral to the Metropolitan Cathedral where the service was concluded. Yet it was no bad thing for our visitors to see just a small passing remnant of the hatred which had marred our city in the past and out of which had been wrested the new spirit of reconciliation and partnership.

We believe that this new spirit is now evident much more widely than just among a select body of enthusiasts for Christian Unity. The Covenant, signed by the Merseyside Church leaders in 1985, has been endorsed since then by each new Church leader accepting office in the area as a replacement for a departing signatory. Indeed our signing of the original Covenant has proved the pattern of partnership between Churches and congregations at a much more local level. As the three Joint Presidents of MARCEA, we have, together with John Newton, witnessed the signing of local Covenants in some fifteen different neighbourhoods in our diocese. In each case there has been important groundwork done by the full-time ecumenical officer who serves all our Churches. This crucial, but often hidden, role has been filled in turn by Baptist, Roman Catholic, Anglican and United Reformed Church clergy. A local Covenant should not be signed until the new relationship and its implications have been carefully thought through. In this way the commitment is not dependent upon an individual priest or minister, who may in time retire or be transferred elsewhere. This preliminary has been a necessary precaution and often proves to be a valuable contribution to the process of building up friendship between the partners, individuals or congregations, and helps to prepare them to face new challenges together. There have been occasions when other Christian groups, such as Christian Fellowships, have entered a local Covenant as associate members. Other Independent Evangelical and Pentecostal Churches have kept their distance from ecumenical structures. But we have tried to act as Christian supporters and friends, whenever that has been possible.

We were especially moved at the signing of the Kirkby Covenant in 1992 between one Methodist Church, three Anglican Churches and seven Roman Catholic Churches. Kirkby is a post-war overspill development from Liverpool. It suffered much deprivation in the 1970s and 1980s, and still comprised many families whose roots lie in Scotland Road and the religious battlegrounds of old. That their various church communities were coming together to sign a Covenant was an astonishing achievement, representing many years of careful preparation, exchange and mutual support in face of industrial and social hardships. So it was full of meaning for us as for the rest of the congregation in a packed Church, when representatives of local communities read a preliminary declaration of intent before signing the act of Covenant.

'We have reflected on the stories of our people,' they said; 'of their common suffering, poverty and joy in the inner city of Liverpool for nearly one hundred years. We have thought again of the exodus which led us together to the new land of Kirkby, and of the fading of old divisive memories and the deepening discovery of our common Christian Faith. Particularly in the past twenty years we have been conscious of the presence of the Spirit, leading us to a sharing in understanding of our various traditions. We have prayed together, worshipped together, given public testimony to our common Faith, and joined steadfastly together to repel attacks on the dignity and helplessness of our people . . .'

It was with very full but thankful hearts that some minutes later we witnessed their signed commitment to God and to one another for the future.

There were great celebrations in Kirkby that evening, and some months later we were glad to share this experience with our friends from Belfast and Glasgow at one of the regular overnight meetings which the Church leaders of all three cities hold twice a year and call 'The North-West Triangle'. When last they came to Liverpool, we made a presentation about what our covenanted partnership had come to mean at local level, and we were able to instance three local Covenants to show what was possible.

Kirkby was one of the three selected, with its recent signing, the fruit of long endeavour. The principal Roman Catholic priest, a well-known pocket dynamo, Canon Jimmy Collins, now in his seventies, who had remained with his people in Kirkby for close on thirty years, was there to speak gently and unassumingly of how out of shared suffering, trust had developed. Formby was another example, where the actual working through of their Covenant had been in process for some years. Lent study courses, justice and peace meetings, youth work provision, and Holy Week witness figured in a very varied programme each year. The third example was from Ditton and Hough Green, on the outskirts of Widnes. They were able to report on one shared Anglican/Roman Catholic Church and one shared Anglican/Methodist Church. Joint pilgrimages, youth and community work, shared preparation for baptism and weddings, and house prayer groups were features of their life. Acts of Covenant and their consequences represent a great deal more than the eloquent illuminated document which usually hangs at the back of a participating Church.

One clergyman, very conscious in his inner-city area of a strong wish not to be disloyal to the past, once told us, 'The fact that you two bishops are so often seen together has given us permission to come together locally.' Once that initial coming together has taken place, local needs soon show the clergy an increasing number of opportunities for joint action. Such sharing of concern leads naturally and without fear to the sharing of prayer. Already people have largely forgotten how total was the segregation, if not alienation, until relatively recently. The Kirkby covenant showed that there were still some who remembered, but had no wish to go back.

One important consequence of our steadily developing partnership has been the general assumption that in matters of common concern it will be possible for the Churches to speak with one voice, or at least to advance one viewpoint. We would have to admit that more often than not ecumenism adds additional demands to our work; but there are occasions when the Churches are quite happy to nominate just one Church representative where our presence or co-operation is requested. Obviously this necessitates mutual trust and good communication between us. It ensures that often duplication of effort can be avoided. One agreed representative can usefully concentrate his attention and interest on a particular project of importance to the general community. It also reduces the danger of one denomination being played off against another; and it adds to the credibility of the witness which is offered in the name of the Churches.

A fair example of this arose when Liverpool was shortlisted among the cities and towns bidding for selection in the first City Challenge competition. This scheme had been introduced by Michael Heseltine in 1991 on his return to political favour and his second term as Secretary of State at the Department of the Environment. Monies customarily spread to meet various urban development schemes had been put together to form a handful of prizes and bids invited for the most promising projects. When the various entries had been shortlisted, the Secretary of State and supporting ministers visited the chosen cities and towns to examine the projects in detail. Their task was also to try to measure the support which might be expected from the private sector and from voluntary and local community organisations.

For Liverpool the visiting Minister was Michael Portillo, who, when he had listened to the official presentation, asked, 'Who speaks for the community?' Harry Rimmer, the leader of the City Council, turned to those who had been gathered in support and prompted the Archbishop to do so. At the conclusion of the submission, the Minister said, 'I cannot think of any other city in this country which would think of producing a bishop to speak in the name of the community.' Subsequently, when the Challenge was awarded to Liverpool, we both agreed to serve on the Forum overseeing the development of different aspects of the bid, while the priest who was the nominee of all the Churches jointly was elected to the small committee to represent the voluntary sector on the executive.

Sometimes one of us can appropriately act for all. As a rule this comes about as a result of careful consultation and planning. When the three of us are to take part in a service for the signing of a local Covenant, we take it in turns as to who preaches, who leads the intercessions and who reads the Scriptures. Wherever suitable – as on occasions when we have figured together on a televised *Songs of Praise* – we join together for the final blessing. But now and then the question of 'Who presides?' is settled by force of circumstances.

DEREK WORLOCK: There are several occasions each year when we all take part together in some service with a particular theme. Among these is an ecumenical peace service which is held in October to mark One World Week. On one occasion it was taking place in the Anglican Cathedral, and the three of us sat side by side with David presiding in the middle. That evening the preacher took rather longer than expected. He was followed by an enthusiastic steel band, which achieved such a response from the congregation that they worked confidently and steadily through their repertoire.

As the clock moved round, John Newton whispered to us both that he had to preach a sermon elsewhere and had quite a journey to make first. He tiptoed out. Ten minutes and several encores later, David informed me that he had an evening service to attend at St Helens. Would I carry on, preside over the last throes of the steel band and give the final blessing? Stray visitors entering the Anglican Cathedral must have been puzzled to find a Roman empurpled prelate presiding from the Bishop's chair.

DAVID SHEPPARD: A return fixture took place in August 1992 at a great ecumenical service in the Metropolitan cathedral to mark the return of the Tall Ships to the Mersey. Controversy emerged when internationally the 1992 race was labelled The Columbus Regatta, provoking a Five Hundred Years of Resistance movement. There had been many months of sensitive negotiations with the City, the Merseyside Development Corporation and Five Hundred Years of Resistance. Derek had been principally engaged in these negotiations on behalf of the three of us, and would normally have presided at the service in our presence.

When the time came, Derek was just recovering from major surgery for cancer and was quite unable to be there. Accordingly, he asked me to preside at this great service and to occupy the Archbishop's Chair. It was part of the fruit of our trusting relationship and friendship that everyone appeared to accept this as entirely natural. They would certainly not have done so when the Cathedral was first built in the 1960s. Later Derek told me how consoled and encouraged he had felt when he did not receive one single letter of complaint or objection.

The close collaboration and the growing trust between the Churches

have made it possible in most matters for the media and public authorities to refer in general terms to 'the Church leaders', even though
that term can cause difficulty for some of the Free Churches. This
development has made the representation of the Christian viewpoint
a great deal easier, for there is seldom either the inclination or the
possibility to advance a series of differing attitudes or teachings. But it
has meant that, without distorting what we see to be the truth, there
must be mutual sensitivity in what is said or written. In some sense
it is a problem which is always with us, but this public expectation
of a common mind has to a great extent come about naturally and
gradually.

After our coming together in Liverpool in 1976, we had been looked
to relatively quickly for the expression of a voice for those not
normally able to make themselves heard. This was a role which
was not self-sought, though we tried from the first to place ourselves
alongside the poor and disadvantaged. It arose in some measure from
the work of reconciliation which came to be expected of us whenever
relationships had broken down. Originally the role of reconciliation was
requested of us in disputes between employers and their workforce, or
between management and trade union. It achieved greater consequence
when the City Council, under Militant leadership, decided on a policy of
confrontation with central Government.

Even before that, it was a role into which we had both been drawn
during the urban riots of 1981. We have described this in some
detail in *Better Together* (chap. 8, 'A Time for Healing'). That was
in many ways the most difficult and demanding time in our years in
Liverpool. It called for a combination of trust and a willingness to accept
misunderstanding and misrepresentation. In our efforts to secure justice
for the oppressed, it was necessary that we show respect for those who
were accustomed to hostility and abuse. Only then were we able to
achieve the trust and co-operation needed as a basis for reconciliation.
But this was not always easily understood by third parties.

At least people knew thereafter where the Church would stand. They
found that the phrase 'Bias to the Poor' was more than just the title of
David's book. It was a standpoint which came to be expected of us,
though we endeavoured to avoid giving the impression of unreasonable
partisanship. But there were few quick solutions, and feelings ran high
at that time. In the memoirs of her *Downing Street Years*, Margaret
Thatcher alludes to our advocacy of Liverpool at that time when the
Government found it difficult to make a positive intervention in a
very complex situation. When finally the Prime Minister succeeded
in visiting Liverpool she did indeed send for various people to meet
her. However, it was not schoolchildren, as she now suggests, but
the leader of Liverpool's black community, Wally Brown, who told
press reporters on the steps of the Town Hall that she had indeed

listened to what he had told her, but she could not be expected to understand.

Such was the alienation gap that progress in working for understanding was inevitably slow. We were summoned to see the Prime Minister that morning, and when she departed some hours later, she took away with her, noted on the back of an envelope, some of our catch-phrases of that time: words we had offered in response to her comments on the situation. 'We want reconciliation not recrimination', we told her and 'You cannot impose a solution on this community: it must be worked out with them.' We were bold enough to remind her that the word 'compassion' was not patronising, as she suggested. 'It means "suffering with",' we told her 'and that is a very important consideration with this community just now.' Most of our pearls were duly produced at a press conference that evening before she returned to London. But somehow that final jewel about compassion, though noted at the time, never reappeared. As Denis Thatcher remarked to her at the time, 'That's not really one of your words, is it?'

Many people in Liverpool have encouraged us to speak up, though we have never tried to act as negotiators. We have no mandate for such a task. More often it has been in the role of communicators between those whose relationship has broken down that our Christian task of reconciliation has led us. Sometimes this has been in the realm of industrial disputes, occasionally in relations between central and local government and, curiously enough, relatively seldom in healing religious differences of a denominational character. An elderly Churchman once remarked that, in his experience, 60 per cent of the problems he encountered were really personality problems. It is suggested that nowadays that is probably an underestimate: not because real differences no longer exist but because now there are established means of sorting out such matters. Above all there is steadily increasing trust and a desire to resolve such differences peaceably.

Some of the matters where our services have been sought, or where we have thought it necessary to challenge in the name of Christ and of social justice, have not always been recognised as religious issues. Not unnaturally we have often found ourselves caught up in the 'Church and Politics' debate. In its most simplistic form, our reply has usually been that God calls us to give practical expression to our love of neighbour. We have never disguised the heavy demands this dimension of our work makes upon our partnership and upon us as individuals. The commitment to respond to such needs is not to be undertaken lightly. Yet it would have been a betrayal of our responsibilities *not* to apply Gospel principles to the needs and injustices afflicting those we have been called to serve in the challenging and stressful years we have been together in Liverpool.

There have been times when swift and specific action has been required of us, and when our expected response would inevitably produce a clash with an existing commitment in the diary of one or both of us. The years have shown a steady increase in the number of demands at national as well as local or community level. We have through experience gradually produced the priorities which guide us. For example, we have tried always to respond positively to an invitation or call for help from Northern Ireland. We have found that generally, when our positive response has depended upon our cancelling a more local commitment, there has been quite remarkable understanding and acceptance of the decision made. But the time needed to deal with a local industrial dispute, where our help or intervention may well be sought, is considerable. Over the years, it has been possible to establish a number of helpers who can advise us and who can confidently take on the job at local level, perhaps after an initial expedition from ourselves to open doors, or at least establish a common desire to reach a solution.

It can be quite a problem, when faced with some unexpected crisis or call for help, to work out whether intervention or response is really called for. Can one of us handle it on his own? Are the time and work of both of us – sometimes all three of us – justified against the more normal demands of our duties? Archbishop Runcie once suggested that our principle of acceptance might well be 'when one and one add up to more than two'. In recent years, especially when promoting ecumenical collaboration elsewhere, we have carried the flag with the help of John Newton as Free Church Moderator. Almost invariably we have found that the additional representative can give added weight to the cause we are preaching. But it takes, not saves time.

The 'Double Act' was not a setpiece for frequent repetition to one audience after another. Often we are asked to speak together about our experience in Liverpool. Question time frequently raises queries about the current public image of our city, often related to the latest television series set in Liverpool, tending to caricature some of our fellow-citizens, portrayed as feckless, shiftless, likeable rogues with scant regard for the law. Hopefully, we have tried without self-righteousness or disguising some local weaknesses to present a more positive picture of a city, in some ways damaged and hurt, but resilient and unwilling to be written off. It was revealing to find how many of our young people felt that a television series such as *Bread*, however amusing, did little to improve their employment prospects.

When preaching or speaking together, we have made a practice of dividing a sermon or address into four parts, with one of us taking parts one and three, and the other parts two and four. This at least makes it clear to those listening that there has been some careful preparation, and that they are not just being treated to two sermons, with one following another in duplication of precisely the same theme. We frequently vary the batting or speaking order, do not hesitate to tease each other in public and, more often than not, avoid stealing each other's anecdotes or jokes.

Our mileage has been extensive: 'in journeyings often', though less frequently since Derek's illness in 1992. Time spent together travelling has proved the opportunity to prepare future joint texts, or at least to deal with the mass of common correspondence. Each of us has to keep a file on his desk to deal with letters affecting both of us or calling for joint action. We exchange in advance each other's diaries of engagements for the week ahead, with accompanying details of addresses and telephone numbers. In this way we ensure the possibility of swift communication and consultation. Partnership of this kind provides good mutual support, but you also need to be convinced of the value of ecumenism and joint service of the community.

When we were together in South Africa in May 1989, at the joint invitation of Archbishop Desmond Tutu and of the then Roman Catholic Archbishop of Cape Town, the late Stephen Naidoo, we spoke together on one occasion to a specially assembled group in the Anglican Cathedral in Cape Town. During the break for lunch, the Anglican dean asked how all this collaboration worked out in practice. The answer we gave was that the wide range of shared activities required us to talk our attitudes and policies through frequently. If we had not had good time alone during the week, the bottom line was probably to spend an hour on the telephone on Sunday night. The Dean's response, in its innocence, was memorable. He thought for a while and then said, 'That's all very well for you, but over here our bishops are all very busy men.'

A realistic approach to the diary is an important factor, if there is to be an adequate response, not only to engagements which can be planned well in advance – which often means a couple of years or more – but also to needs and circumstances quite beyond our control. If it is difficult for one bishop to find a hole in his diary, it is considerably more difficult where two already full diaries are concerned. Even with our quite different agendas, it helps to have some common priorities, especially where changes of commitment are required. We try not to be unreasonable in our expectations of one another. After several years we are reasonably adept at anticipating each other's likely reaction and reading each other's minds. This was a hard lesson learned from one of our earliest joint commitments.

DEREK WORLOCK: When, quite soon after our coming to Liverpool, it was announced that Dunlop would close its large plant at Speke, at a cost of several thousand jobs, the shop-stewards came to seek our help. They claimed that the management was unwilling to discuss the matter with them, and therefore asked us to join them in a protest 'march for jobs' through the city of Liverpool to Pier Head the following Saturday. I was clear about the priority for myself, and all my instincts knew that it was important for the Church Leaders to be seen acting together on this occasion. I therefore decided rather rashly to take a risk and I told the shop-stewards that I would be there with them and that the other Church Leaders would be there as well.

DAVID SHEPPARD: In fact there was nothing straightforward about it where I was concerned. Of course I shared and agreed with the priority, but I had to make an awkward decision as to how to free myself from my Diocesan Synod which was meeting that Saturday morning. To join the protest march I would have to leave my meeting half-way through, and thereby miss a debate and vote on a diocesan post which I considered of much importance. I decided to risk this, and explained to the Synod where I felt the priorities of the Kingdom would want me to be. In the event the vote was narrowly lost, almost certainly influenced by feelings that bishops had no business to be joining a demonstration in preference to carrying out accepted Church business. While the march did not reverse the decision to close Dunlop's, the management undertook to meet the men's representatives two days later, agreeing to some improvements in redundancy terms.

Our presence at the front of the march did not speak of worldly power; but it did show that we wanted to stand with people at great moments of human need. Our appearance at the head of the protesters, alongside trade union leaders and Members of Parliament, caused quite a stir at the time, though in the years that have followed it would be taken for granted. Perhaps the difference is that for some years now it seems to have been accepted by both management and shopfloor that, where closures and heavy loss of jobs are concerned, it has been useful for one party or both to alert us before the issue becomes public. In this way we may be of help in the task of reconciliation, or negotiation, or just the raising of morale in a threatened workforce, while its leaders try to negotiate the best possible terms or to save the maximum number of jobs.

That decision to stand together with the Dunlop marchers, and to give that cause preference over attendance at a Synod, reflected our shared belief that the mission of the Church is not primarily to care for our own condition of life, but by our life to bear a witness which may bring the Gospel to the world. God's rule is not just about filling churches but about reaching out to touch the whole world.

At the heart of the teaching of Jesus in the Gospels are the parables and statements about the Kingdom of God. The German theologian, Hans Küng, summarises the meaning of the Kingdom as Creation Healed. That identifies the saving role of Christ in the world of today.

It also shows the particular concern of the followers of Christ for the disadvantaged, for those who have been hurt in some way. It recognises what some see as social and political issues, as in fact being 'faith-issues', involving people's dignity, love of neighbour, and the use or waste of God-given abilities. We have to believe that in his Kingdom, the Creator-God is concerned with the quality of life which all human beings experience. As citizens of the Kingdom, and followers of Christ, we must strive to reflect that same concern together. At heart that has guided the pattern of our partnership.

2

From Confrontation to Co-operation

In the autumn of 1993, the European Institute of Urban Affairs of the Liverpool John Moores University was invited to make an evaluation of the various projects being given effect as a result of Liverpool's successful bid for the City Challenge award. Particular attention was to be given to the various partnerships set up between public- and private-sector interests. Had the much publicised conflicts and industrial tensions of the past been overcome? How real was the collaboration needed if the planners' dreams were to come true?

In many ways the exercise was to be attempted too soon, but this early stage monitoring was to be welcomed, even if only to counter the steady flow of Sunday newspaper reports on aspects of Liverpool life and its economy. Over the years these had proved to be at best highly selective, mostly critical and almost invariably sensational. On the whole the evaluation carried out by the Institute of Urban Affairs gave good grounds for hope. The report itself revealed a degree of background knowledge which was a necessary factor in any assessment; and it explained without attempting to excuse. Any tendency in that direction leads to the all too easy charge of 'whingeing again'.

The authors of the Report, Professor Michael Parkinson and Mrs Hilary Russell, wrote:

> The creation of institutional partnerships is a particular challenge for Liverpool. Until relatively recently decision-making in the city was characterised by an obvious lack of partnership between the city council and the government, the city council and the private sector, the city council and the community. The political difficulties and uncertainties of the last decade are mainly past. The efforts of Business Opportunities on Merseyside (BOOM), the emergence of the Mersey Partnership and the City Centre Partnership all testify to the substantial efforts being made within the city to

25

create partnerships. City Challenge is one important attempt to complement those initiatives . . . (*Liverpool City Challenge. First Report of Independent Evaluation Team*, Section 3, 1993).

The Report went on to point out that these were early days, and that some of the attitudes formed during the difficult period of the mid-1980s had still to be overcome. Nevertheless the moves were in the right direction and gave ground for hope that present co-operation would bear fruit. This same spirit of co-operation was noted in a leading article in *The Times* (12 November 1993) which remarked that 'there are signs that some regions are moving beyond the old polarity between town hall and quango to develop their own alliances and collaborative ventures'. It pointed to the example of the recently launched Mersey Partnership, which would co-ordinate marketing strategy for Liverpool and its surrounding region. 'Liverpool' said the leader writer, 'is being transformed by new policies of co-operation between governing authorities and the academic, business and church communities.' If that were not praise enough – and change enough for *The Times* – the article concluded: 'It is heartening that in many areas, public and private sector are now collaborating unbidden by Whitehall, and are treating public funds as investment rather than subsidy.'

It was a long time since such recognition had come from that particular source. Now we read: 'Old tensions between business and local government are slowly relaxing. The word "partnership" has been used so indiscriminately in political discourse that it has become almost meaningless. But in the context of local governance, it deserves to be reclaimed.'

It was a welcome, if unexpected, recognition of the spirit of co-operation which has been the watchword of local Government in Liverpool during the last five or six years, since those anxious times of confrontation under the Militants. In effect it has meant that the City Council, under a moderate Labour leadership, has had to accept and to make the most of partnership with a Conservative Government in Westminster. It has meant working within government policies, even when on occasion these have required unpalatable job losses and putting major services out to contract. Such pragmatism has not been unprincipled. Those bearing the responsibility of leadership during this period have known well that the people they represent had suffered enough from the consequences of the deliberate policy of their Militant predecessors who, between 1983 and 1987, brought the city to the brink of bankruptcy. To some it had seemed very brave for Derek Hatton and his colleagues to proclaim 'no cuts in jobs or services'. But budgets have to be balanced. If they are ignored, future years have to be spent trying to catch up; paying back loans to foreign banks denies the resources then required to meet pressing needs. This was a lesson which during those years Liverpool learned at considerable cost.

The Militant leadership of the former council chose to 'go for broke', in order to make a decisive impact on housing needs. 'Hatton's houses', as they were called, are still quite a popular legacy of this period in some of the neediest areas. On the credit side, some 4,000 well-built council houses were produced at a time when Government policies had cut back virtually all Council house-building. In spite of Government policy, the City Council chose to pursue its Urban Regeneration Programme: indeed it let some Government grants go by default, because they did not fit in with their priorities. But there was a price to pay, not only from the animosity aroused in Whitehall, but in the consequence of transferring all available monies to the house-building programme. Other aspects of community need were neglected.

During the week following the removal from office of forty-seven Militant councillors, the new Labour Chairman of Housing told us of the situation which he had inherited. Four thousand good homes had indeed been built, but money intended for regular maintenance had been diverted, with the result that for four years no repairs had been carried out to the other sixty-four thousand dwellings rented from the City Council. Repairs had already been underfunded for years. The hard truth was that during the so-called Militant years, despite all the claims about protecting jobs and services, services were in fact not maintained. Funds were diverted. Hence the reports about vacant posts not being filled, and about schoolchildren lacking even exercise books in which to write.

In *Better Together* (chap. 10, 'Two Nations') we have already told in some detail the story of Liverpool's Rates Crisis in the mid-1980s, and of the clash between central Government and the City Council, the majority of whose Labour members stood firm with the relatively small but vocal Militant Tendency leadership. There is no point in repeating this detailed account here, though it is impossible for us to reflect on our years in Merseyside without some assessment of those dark days when the City Council defied the equally confrontational policy pursued by Margaret Thatcher's Government, of breaking the power of local authorities. The legal process whereby the Councillors appealed against the penalties imposed by the District Auditor teetered on until March 1987, when some forty-seven of the Councillors were surcharged heavily and personally disqualified from holding office. Some of these men, who in solidarity had mistakenly supported what was a disastrous policy, had a fine record of public service. We did not hesitate to acknowledge this in a joint public statement, in which we also criticised the system of personal surcharge of individual councillors. We understood why some Liverpool people felt so disregarded that confrontation seemed the only route to being heard with any effect.

But our reflection is that the Militant-led policy of confrontation proved disastrous for the most vulnerable people in the city.

All this background has to be kept in mind in attempting any evaluation of the present policy of co-operation, and the development of partnerships, adopted by the moderate Labour Council, led in the last few years by Councillor Harry Rimmer. It was not an easy or immediate transition. It was evident that the trust of the civil servants in Whitehall had been forfeited by their finger-burning experience with the Militants. Indeed in our opinion one of the most dangerous aspects of the Rates Crisis was when the Government gave active consideration to the appointment of Commissioners to run Liverpool after the disqualification of the Council. The lesson of Northern Ireland and of the abolition of Stormont in favour of direct rule from Westminster was all too clear. How nearly this took place in Liverpool historians will judge.

In his account of *The Turbulent Years*, Kenneth Baker, then Minister of State with responsibility for Local Government, and from September 1985 Secretary of State for the Environment, writes of the 'Doomsday scenario' where the Government would have to appoint Commissioners who would run all Liverpool's services including education, old people's homes and refuse collection. Recalling the winter 1985/86, Baker writes:

> We set about trying to find people who could do this, but it was clear that Commissioners would need the protection of the police and armed forces . . . The Commissioners would become very unpopular as they implemented policies to restore Liverpool's financial balance. It was a miserable job, and as we considered the various candidates the shortlist became shorter and shorter and actually narrowed down to one person . . .

In the end it was decided by a special committee under Margaret Thatcher to 'take no action until services had actually broken down as a result of Militant action, for local people would then appreciate the appalling chaos and demand that the Government act. This policy was known as "Five minutes past midnight"' (Kenneth Baker, *The Turbulent Years* (Faber & Faber, 1993), chap.5.) Kenneth Baker refers to our role of communicating and consulting with both parties in this dispute. In those consultations we firmly opposed the appointment of Commissioners. Reflecting after the lapse of years, we comment with regret that some of the powers that would then have been taken over by Commissioners have since been transferred from local authorities to central Government, notably in the case of education.

The Rates Crisis of 1985/87 eventually reached its climax with the disqualification of roughly half of the City Council. By that time Kenneth Baker had taken his reforming zeal to the Department of Education and we found ourselves having to deal with yet one more Secretary of State for the Environment, with special responsibility for Merseyside. In 1981 Margaret Thatcher had listened to our requests during the riots that there be a minister in the Cabinet with responsibility for Merseyside, who would be the focus of the many different approaches which would have to be made, and who in turn would represent Government policy to an area which felt alienated from much of the rest of the nation. In response she appointed Michael Heseltine as Minister for Merseyside, and his activities in succeeding months are still remembered with gratitude in Liverpool.

In the twelve years which have followed it has been difficult to keep pace with the appropriate office-holders. We have tried to keep in touch personally with each minister holding this special prime responsibility for Merseyside, though the 'clout' of a minister within the Cabinet has given way to the exercise of influence by a more junior minister or Parliamentary Under-Secretary in the Department of the Environment. In twelve years that has meant meeting (sometimes in Liverpool, often in Westminster) with Michael Heseltine, Tom King, Patrick Jenkin, Kenneth Baker, Nicholas Ridley, David Hunt, David Trippier, Chris Patten, Michael Heseltine again, Michael Portillo, Robert Key, and currently Robin Squire. The quick turn-round says something about commitment as well as about government policy. In the most recent Cabinet and ministerial reshuffle, all three Department of the Environment ministers were moved elsewhere. The sponsor minister for the Merseyside region is currently in the Department for Education. Though our contact with some has obviously been short term, many of them became personally our good friends.

There was a period, following Derek Hatton's confrontation with the unfortunate Patrick Jenkin, who had made every effort to achieve a solution to the Rates Crisis, when even civil servants in Westminster were cautious about the re-establishment of communications. Some Secretaries of State were sadly reluctant to assume the tainted title 'Minister for Merseyside'. We have the word of the Chief Constable that after that unhappy episode and the disqualification of the City Councillors, no single Government Minister visited Liverpool over a period of some eighteen months. So Nicholas Ridley's identification of the city with what he termed 'the loony left' did not help. Nor did we escape his rapier tongue when at last he agreed to meet us in his office at the Department of the Environment on 23 July 1986. The date and place of this first meeting were significant, as they coincided with the wedding at that precise moment of HRH the Duke of York in nearby Westminster Abbey. As a result the Department in Marsham Street and its approaches were sealed off for security purposes and it was with difficulty that we walked a considerable distance, talking our way through numerous police barriers before – after a cooling-off period in the waiting room – we were admitted to the Secretary of State's presence.

The encounter was memorable. Nicholas Ridley rose and, wreathed in cigarette smoke, demanded of us: 'How do I know which of you is which?' We each identified the other and were asked what we wanted. We had in fact had to submit in advance an agenda for discussion. 'We want to ask you' Derek said, 'whether you are in fact the new Minister for Merseyside whom the Prime Minister has promised us.' Mr Ridley's reply also was memorable, delivered after a deep draw on his cigarette, 'Well' he said slowly, 'I understand I am responsible for every town, city, village and hamlet in this country, not to mention every butterfly and dog licence, so I don't see why that should not include Merseyside.' Then David decided to take over a conversation which was not proving promising. 'I read in the *Guardian* a few days ago,' he said, perhaps leading with his chin, 'that you had expressed doubt about any particular commitment to Merseyside. Do you accept that we do have special needs?' With that Nicholas Ridley rose from his chair in angry protest. 'I regard that remark as quite unacceptable. It's moral blackmail.'

The rest of the meeting, which lasted another fifteen minutes, did not really improve on the high quality of this beginning. It proved to be in marked contrast with a discussion some months later to which the Secretary of State was bidden by Mrs Thatcher, who had invited us to Downing Street to discuss the likely aftermath of the approaching disqualification of Militant Councillors in Liverpool. 'Keep in touch with Nick Ridley,' she told us. 'He should be our contact.' She beamed at us, while the Minister for Merseyside pushed his spectacles back up his aquiline nose.

Different days. To be fair, Nicholas Ridley did visit our city on several occasions before he departed for Trade and Industry in the summer of 1989. But his 'loony left' label did untold harm to the image of Liverpool for several years after he had shed responsibility for Merseyside – alongside the butterflies and dog licences.

A good example of this was the Walton by-election following the death of that doughty fighter for Liverpool, Eric Heffer. In June 1991 the media descended on the city in considerable strength and there was a daily visit from one or other senior Conservative minister who, faced with inevitable defeat in the by-election, used the occasion to smear the city's record, especially in local government. There was a dispute at the time over refuse collection, with rotting garbage in the streets. The threat to close cemeteries revived memories of the winter of discontent in 1978/79. All the choicest Ridley epithets were produced daily. The 'mainstream Labour' group, under Councillor Rimmer, battled on with only a handful more votes than the hardline 'Broad Left', who at one time seemed likely to be the sole beneficiaries of the campaign being waged by the Tory visitors to the by-election battleground. By chance, Channel 4 had just run the drama series *GBH* by the Liverpool writer Alan Bleasdale. In this series, a populist left-wing leader was portrayed in a way which many took to be a description of Liverpool in its years of Militant leadership. No city can quickly change its image once it has been so smeared.

After one of us had been provoked in a radio interview into appealing to members of the Cabinet to stop using our city as a political football for party political purposes, we decided, together with John Newton, to issue a statement affirming 'the courage of the present leadership of the City Council in trying to pull the city out of its deep-set financial problems'. We regretted that comments from outside the City seemed 'calculated only to make political capital out of what most of us knew was bound to be a rough period in carrying through necessary but unpopular decisions, including some job cuts'. The result of the by-election was important for the City Council as well as for the national image of Merseyside. Lesley Mahmood, standing for extremist 'Liverpool Labour' against the official Labour candidate, Peter Kilfoyle, who had played a major part in expelling Militants from the Labour Party, was overwhelmingly defeated. For a while at least it proved a turning-point, and in subsequent years Harry Rimmer has succeeded in maintaining his balancing act. In 1993 the City's budget was passed without the brinkmanship of each previous year We began to ride more easily those taunts about the 'loony left'. It began to be recognised, as *The Times* leader admitted, that there were good things to be learned from Liverpool. But the image of the place and its people has remained crucial.

To what extent has the Merseyside image changed in these last years, and with what justification? As early as 1988, we began to hear people in other parts of the country saying somewhat tentatively, 'We hear that things are a bit better in Liverpool – aren't they?' Often it was the expression of genuine interest, but without much information about the alleged improvement. We were able to give a rather guarded reply about both good news and bad news: good news that business confidence is growing, but bad news that some of the benefits which have come to the city in one way or another still seem to bring little benefit to a number of high-unemployment areas, especially in the perimeter estates. We had no wish to deny or impair the improved image of the city, but we could not ignore continuing long-term unemployment and areas of widespread poverty.

The implementation of Liverpool's City Challenge has recently done much to improve the image for our visitors, as have spectacular events such as the Return of the Tall Ships to Merseyside in 1992 and the fiftieth anniversary of the conclusion of the Battle of the Atlantic in 1993. At such times of course the great buildings of the city are seen to great advantage. Clearly considerable efforts have been made to restore our architectural heritage and with it, our pride. But it still remains true that visitors, asked what has impressed them most on such an occasion, often reply: 'The spirit of the people.' This is admittedly frequently given a considerable boost by the celebration in question, especially if the event is accorded good publicity in the media. Sadly this is not automatic, nor widespread: unless of course it is a tragedy or a cause of shame. The football disasters of Heysel and Hillsborough were examples of this, and newsreel film of these events is regularly repeated as a background to a Liverpool story.

When the terrible murder of two-year-old James Bulger was reported in 1993, the tabloid Press wrote of Kirkby as though most of its inhabitants were criminals. The fact that the young victim and his parents happened to live there was the only connection with Kirkby. The crime was committed and the young killers lived in Walton, not even in the same borough. At the time of the binmen's strike in 1991, one quality newspaper produced a composite picture of a huge mound of rubbish taken elsewhere and superimposed over a background picture of Liverpool's Liver Buildings. At the same time, a photographer from a tabloid newspaper instructed a group of nine-year-old boys in Toxteth to run towards the camera, shaking their fists and looking as angry and violent as they could. In this way he was able to project the image of Liverpool as his editor wanted it. A final example would be the quite splendid commemoration of the Battle of the Atlantic, when thousands of those veteran heroes of seamen marched through our streets. All the newspapers turned up for the occasion but the photographers' only interest was the presence together of the Prince of Wales and Princess Diana, and the latter's struggle with her picture hat and short skirt, as the wind billowed around the Anglican Cathedral where the official service was being held.

To change an image of impoverished, irresponsible hooliganism is not easy. It must be 'newsworthy', one is told, and it takes patience and perseverance to tell the positive story which will interest the media. But some will pick it up, often when least expected. It is difficult to work out priorities when the unexpected, demanding personal presence or instant comment breaks in upon an already settled, crowded programme. Sometimes one has to cover for both of us. We go to some lengths to produce joint comments wherever possible. This has sometimes meant a series of long-distance, even international, phone calls, with the help now of the blessed FAX machine. Even joint statements are vulnerable to cuts by the blue pencil of sub-editors, who do not always ascribe as much value to ecumenical partnership as we do. A joint photograph makes it more difficult for a newspaper to give the impression that only one Church is speaking up. Even a joint photo is at risk of dismemberment: once a photo of the three Liverpool

Church leaders had John Williamson, then Free Church Moderator, cut off in his prime, leaving just the two of us in the picture. Because of that experience, we have subsequently encouraged him and his successor, John Newton, to stand between us for a photo call.

The visual image remains important and occasionally efforts to get this right prove successful. The Battle of the Atlantic commemoration – we had to be careful to avoid the word 'celebration' – produced an excellent television documentary from Brian Redhead, and a Supplement from *The Times* revealing in some detail the growth of business confidence in the City. But twice lately we have had to endure misrepresentation by MPs on the south coast, alleging that the source of their rise in local crime rate could be traced from the Liverpool accents of the perpetrators. Such a charge is both unfair and unprovable; and it seems to suggest that more of our young people followed the earlier injunction from Norman Tebbit to 'get on their bikes' in search of a job than proved to be the case. It ignores also the Merseyside Police figures showing that in recent years the crime rate in these parts has been falling. Once again the true image is smeared, and it does have repercussions in trade, industry and employment.

At one of the monthly breakfast meetings of the Michaelmas Group of senior business people – a group which we first brought together in September 1984 – there was a lively discussion of this issue of the image of Merseyside. One member reported that while there was some progress in restoring the true image of the city and its people, we should take note that there was a time bomb ticking away which would blow the better picture into smithereens. He was referring to the independent enquiry into race relations in Liverpool, chaired by Lord Gifford in 1989. In the discussion which followed we tried to explain that while we shared the common desire of the members to publicise a more positive account of our city, we could not be party to a policy which silenced the most disadvantaged sector of our fellow-citizens. To do so would be almost to encourage the development of a ghetto, whose members would be inaudible and possibly invisible. Telling the truth about Liverpool – and indeed about most large cities – must mean telling a Tale of Two Cities, Enterprise City and Hurt City. In making any evaluation it was necessary to look at the whole picture.

Our calling gives us a very privileged viewpoint, from which we cannot separate Christian values, any more than we can exclude personal morality from the concerns of the 'Back to Basics' campaign, waged at the end of 1993. Our belief in God as the Father of all has to come into any attempted evaluation of the state of the nation or of a particular region. He is the Creator and Sustainer of the whole, desiring reliable conditions in which people can develop the particular gifts given to individuals and groups. He calls us to be co-creators, responsible sustainers of the world around us. He is concerned for the whole body, especially for its weakest members, and for those who find themselves left out of good opportunities. He longs to see the gifts he has given to all developed and set free. He cares about the quality of life of all his children, and wants to see the wealth of the whole increased for the common good.

In Coventry Cathedral there is a sculpture of a modern city – skyscrapers, offices, factories, parks, law courts, schools, churches – over which hangs a builder's plumb-line. The idea comes from the Old Testament prophet Amos, with his passion for justice. Amos was popular enough when he pronounced God's judgment against the iniquities of the surrounding nations; but a shock went through his hearers when he described his vision of a 'plumb-line' in the midst of his people, Israel (cf. Amos 7:7–9). Against the plumb-line of God's justice, he saw the actions and attitudes of people of influence as being like crooked, unreliable buildings.

We have seen whole areas which have benefited from various projects of regeneration, especially those in the city centre near the river, but we cannot overlook the other aspect of life in the perimeter estates and, for example, among Liverpool black people. Our plumb-line indicates that we must not ignore the weaker members of the one body: that we must take wealth creation seriously, but also the redistribution of wealth which would open the doors of opportunity more widely. Urban life is full of choices for some of us, but for others it is like a series of doors clanging shut in their faces. Opportunity or deprivation seldom result from one single issue, such as housing or jobs. Rather they result from a confusing interlocking of housing, jobs, health-care, schooling, transport, and access to decision-makers. Some people know that there is room for them in the general provision of the community. Others know all too well that they rarely get past the doors of exclusion.

When it appeared – its likely conclusions had been widely leaked beforehand which undoubtedly lessened their general impact – the Gifford Report attracted most publicity for its comments on relations between the police and the black community. The unofficial nature of the Commission had meant that most police officers felt unable to give evidence, which in turn meant that the Report had significant limitations. Witnesses gave their evidence and were cross-examined in public, which also brought limitations. Nevertheless deep criticism of policing in Liverpool 8 came from a number of witnesses, including 'priests, lawyers, shopkeepers, fire officers, academics, lay visitors, magistrates, councillors, social workers, as well as many ordinary people, black and white, old and young'. Community police were seen as being very fair, but attitudes and actions of the enforcement arm were not regarded as always even-handed. We met Lord Gifford privately and agreed to submit some comments in writing. When the report was published our advisers in the area told us both quite plainly that its findings did not 'go over the top'. They were confident that the evidence had been carefully checked (*Loosen the Shackles: First Report of the Liverpool 8 Inquiry into Race Relations in Liverpool*, Karia Press, 1989).

Since the publication of the report in 1989, the Merseyside Police have undoubtedly tried to make themselves more accessible and to build up more trusting community relations. An increasing number of voices from within the black community have insisted that they genuinely want good communications with the police. When joy-riders killed two children in the streets of Toxteth, mothers banded together to barricade whole streets and demanded greater presence and protection from the police. Much crime in Toxteth, as in other parts of Merseyside and indeed throughout the country, has been drug-related. Most local people will neither condone nor cover up the presence of the drug dealers. When arrests are to be made by an early-morning raid, a senior officer will very likely stand on the pavement outside to explain to local residents what is happening.

There is little doubt that community police have been generally welcomed, especially when that has meant 'the bobby on the beat'. Trying to get close to the community in other ways has had mixed success. In a brave effort the police endeavoured to set up a Police and Community resource centre in the Granby area. They quickly accepted the local designation of 'Cop-shop' and initially its very presence possibly had a salutary effect. One could have little but admiration for the police who staffed it for twenty-four hours a day and endeavoured to be on the friendliest terms with those who called in. Yet some leaders of the local community seem to have given it a wide berth. The building itself was renovated and adapted for use by other agencies which might provide information, advice and services to the local community. To attract customers the Centre even installed a chiropody service but, alas, from many of the residents of the area there seems to have been a boycott.

In answer to an invitation from the police themselves, we called one afternoon to witness the Centre in action. It was alleged later that many of those who called in had been encouraged to do so, but the efforts of the police concerned were most commendable. There were signs that it was beginning to contribute to the greater sense of security and the reduction of tension in the area. Another body taking away some of the sense of powerlessness is MBO (Merseyside Broad Based Organising). This is chiefly made up of groups based on Churches and other religious organisations. Through Community Organising it seeks to maintain a rolling programme of actions across the city, rather than the spasmodic eruptions of community indignation over one local issue. In spite of all these different initiatives, detectable progress in Police and Community relations remains slow and subject to setbacks. A few weeks after our visit to the 'Cop-shop' in Granby Street, the premises were rammed by a burning vehicle. Afterwards a new protective barrier was erected and the praiseworthy initiative was continued. Current criticism is that the staffing of the 'Cop-shop' takes bobbies off the beat where they are most needed to deter drug dealers.

Clearly there is need for perseverance in a delicate and frequently changing situation. Recently there was a police recruitment drive, and some seventy persons turned up at an Open Day, arranged by the Merseyside Police and the agency South Liverpool Personnel. Eighteen candidates embarked on a pre-recruitment course. And they will have a good chance of being accepted for entry into the police force. All are from Liverpool 8, nine of them black, a mixture of men and women. Such a development would have been unthinkable a few years ago. Recently Merseyside Police told us that in 1987 there were thirteen police officers from ethnic minorities. In 1994 there were seventy.

The Gifford Report also took a look at the 1984 Race and Housing in Liverpool Report, prepared by the Commission for Racial Equality. Black people were shown not to be offered the more desirable properties in a survey of nominees decided by the Council for Housing Association dwellings: 62 per cent of white applicants obtained centrally heated property, and 25 per cent with its own garden. These figures must be set against 35 per cent and 6 per cent where black people were concerned, even though most of them have lived in Liverpool for long periods, if not all their lives. White nominees were shown to be over four times more likely than black nominees to receive new-build property (*Race and Housing in Liverpool*, Commission for Racial Equality, 1984).

A central recommendation of the CRE Report was that the City Council should monitor the ethnic origin of people applying for housing and being rehoused. The Militant leadership of that time explicitly refused to take steps to monitor their policies. They claimed that they had put into effect new policies which did not discriminate, and that therefore there was no need to monitor. The truth was that their dogma alleged that class, not race, was the decisive factor in disadvantage. Subsequently, the new administration assured the CRE's follow-up enquiry that each applicant for housing was now being asked to complete an ethnic monitoring form. It was our firm belief that the subtle processes of discrimination would only be defeated if there was this careful monitoring. In recent years there is no doubt that the City Council has made strenuous and genuine efforts, through its racial monitoring staff, to remove discrimination from its housing policies.

After the Toxteth riots of 1981, with the other Merseyside Church leaders we played some part in the launch of the Liverpool 8 Law Centre, of which we are joint Presidents. In spite of difficulties in obtaining funding and the cutbacks in access to Legal Aid, the Law

Centre has endured. A wide range of people, many of whom had never thought that the law might be a friend, have found sensitive advice and good legal recommendations at the Law Centre. In *Ten Years On*, Dave Clay, a former Chairman of the Management Committee, brought together an extensive account of the experiences of Liverpool black people between 1981 and 1991. It provides another aspect to any evaluation. He wrote, 'In a city that has no black Headteachers and very few black teachers in general – and in a city where black people have been established for hundreds of years and still face every kind of discrimination – who can talk about development?'

In fact some fresh resources have been targeted at Liverpool 7 and 8 through the Granby Task Force (an offshoot of the Government's Merseyside Task Force) and the European Poverty Three programme. These may seem to be providing relatively small returns, but *should* not be despised for that. The Charles Wootton Centre offers an increasing number of black people Further Education. Housing projects like the Steve Biko Housing Association have been established. But the truth is that access to high-quality jobs, education and housing still seem very elusive to black people in Liverpool. Recently an Access to Law course has been established at Liverpool John Moores University for some twenty-eight students. This could pave the way for the first solicitors and barristers from Liverpool 8.

For another more hopeful sign we may point to the CARE project (Churches' Action for Racial Equality) which is supported by MARCEA. The Merseyside Churches directly fund two workers for the project. Apart from the post of the Ecumenical Officer, these are the only posts directly funded through the Ecumenical Assembly. CARE offers educational programmes to schools and to Churches throughout our region. It has won the confidence of many Liverpool black people, but generally speaking there is very little of the vigorous life of black-led Churches such as may be found in cities where there has been more recent migration.

At the request of an Ecumenical group committed to economic empowerment of the black community, David joined with Bishop Wilfred Wood in giving their names to the Wood–Sheppard Principles. He is co-operating with CARE Project in inviting Liverpool employers to commit themselves to these equal opportunities principles: these include the challenge to regular monitoring of applications for jobs and promotion, to persevering in offers of appropriate training.

Thankfully the British National Party has had little or no success in Liverpool. By and large poor people in Toxteth, black and white, get on together remarkably peacefully. Yet racist assumptions, perhaps unconscious, are deeply entrenched here: the black community continues to find more blocks in the way of good opportunities in jobs, education and housing in Liverpool than in any other British city. The conclusion to a Liverpool seminar on Community Action for Positive Policing, held in October 1992, stated: 'It is too easy for black communities to be marginalised, because the general public are blind to the problems which black people face.' Many white people, including church members, express incredulity when black people explain to them just how real are the blocks in the way of their progress.

Black membership of all the Churches remains small. Perhaps that reflects the sense of a long-established black community which at least until recently was not expected, or did not expect, to have any real say in a white-run organisation. Unfortunately the difficulty of finding opportunities in Inner-City areas and parishes is often compounded by the lack of confidence and fear within black people themselves that they will be rejected.

DAVID SHEPPARD: The Church of England Committee for Black Anglican Concerns paid a two-day visit to Liverpool diocese. In a meeting at the end of the visit they encouraged us to target suitable black people when, for example, school Governors were needed – not wring our hands that nobody came forward in response to a general appeal. One black woman in her sixties told this meeting in Bishop's Lodge that she had been brought up in Liverpool with the understanding that black people should keep quiet. She described how in recent years her Christian faith had grown much stronger: with that growth, she said, she had realised the importance for her of speaking up as a black person.

DEREK WORLOCK: Some twelve years ago I spotted a young man, a true son of Toxteth, who took part in our ecumenical youth pilgrimage. He seemed a born leader, though with little prospect of a job later on because of his background and limited schooling. Eventually, I went to him in Lourdes where he was working with the sick pilgrims. I talked about the Church and vocations and then challenged him: 'Bernie, I want you for the priesthood,' I said. 'Oh no Father,' he replied, 'I couldn't do that.' We laughed and I threatened to pray him into a vocation. Two years later I found his name on a list of candidates for interview. He was willing to give it a try. It meant three years of basic learning at a special college, then six years at the diocesan seminary. The joint difficulty was to get him to raise his sights and believe it possible, and to get his teachers to raise their sights for him. Academically and in every other way he has made it. The real test was when he was placed in an inner-city parish for pastoral experience just before he was due for Holy Orders. When I asked him how he had got on, he replied 'Brilliant, I loved it.' 'What was good about it?' I asked. 'The people,' he replied. 'They seemed to like my sermons, laughed at my jokes, and even applauded the first time.' 'And visiting?' I asked. That could have been the test of acceptance. He went on: 'When I knocked on the first door, it opened on the chain, and an old lady looked out cautiously.' It seemed she recognised his face and his grin. 'Are you from St Michael's?' she asked. He nodded, the chain fell, an arm grabbed him and the voice said, 'Then come inside.' 'And then?' I asked, perhaps unnecessarily. I received the authentic answer. 'Brilliant,' he said.

One small step.

3

A Tale of Two Cities

As a Foreword to the show-book collection of Alex Laing's magnificent photographs of *Liverpool: Images of a Great Seaport* (Editions Limited, Bluecoat Chambers, Liverpool, 1989), Deirdre Murphy writes that 'Liverpool is a city that should be approached from the water. As you cross the great grey width of the River Mersey to the towers on the metropolitan shore, you begin to get the feel of the place and a sense of what has made it. Like Venice it is wedded to the sea.' Despite the magnificent buildings and immense warehouses, now restored and a huge tourist attraction, this romantic allusion to Renaissance art and opulence is not necessarily the first description which leaps to the minds of most Liverpudlians today. Nor is it likely to have done so in the past: not even in the days of Liverpool's greatest repute as a seaport.

We are often reminded that when at the beginning of this century there were more millionaire merchants in Liverpool than in any other part of the country apart from London, the city also possessed the greatest poverty and most extensive overcrowded slums. This division between the very rich and the very poor was reflected in the city's housing, employment and not infrequently sectarian politics. 'Alienation' may have been a new word for the media in describing the Toxteth riots of 1981, but it was not a new feature in the life of the city. So when in recent years we have been asked about improving conditions in Liverpool and the life of its citizens, it has seemed natural enough to reply, 'Well, it's a tale of two cities.'

Many great cities are divided by a river. Often there are profound differences on either side. These can be of a social nature, in the trade or commerce practised, in the quality of the housing and the prosperity of the inhabitants. Relationships between such divided communities depend much on communications and on the existence of a single or unitary authority. The unifying authority of the Merseyside County Council fell victim to the legislation designed to rid the Thatcher

41

Government of Ken Livingstone and the Greater London Council. Established in the 1970s, it was barely given the opportunity to prove its value. Its demise was a severe blow to the various endeavours being made at that time to promote the regeneration of the region as a whole, on both sides of the River Mersey. The splendid results of the Merseyside Development Corporation, established at much the same time, may have changed almost beyond recognition the appearance of the waterfront on the Liverpool side of the river, together with major plans for the Birkenhead side. It was no part of its brief to take Merseyside County Council's place in giving a unifying sense of belonging to one travel-to-work region with its two tunnels and the world-famous 'Ferry across the Mersey'.

A high proportion of the more successful business or professional people still earn their living in Liverpool and cross back each evening to their homes in Cheshire and the Wirral peninsula. A slowly but steadily decreasing number of men and women living in Liverpool's docklands still cross regularly to Birkenhead. It is true that a few of those used to crossing from the Wirral have grown tired of the steadily rising toll-fares for the Mersey tunnels, and have begun to occupy the apartments in the one-time wharf-buildings of Wapping and the Albert Dock: but often only from Monday to Friday. The fate of those in Liverpool's docklands has been different. Some have been fortunate enough to secure decent new housing from the Local Authority or Housing Associations and Co-operatives. But always, much depends upon employment prospects in an area which in the past boasted its walk-to-work opportunities, now sadly diminished.

When we come to assess the effect of programmes aimed at regenerating the city, it becomes important to distinguish between the City Centre and the Inner City, often assumed in English cities to be multi-racial. 'The City Centre' is certainly the hub of the Merseyside region and of Liverpool itself, with another smaller hub across the river in Birkenhead. The city of Liverpool, lying against the Mersey like half a wheel, is virtually fan-shaped, though with ragged edges. Confusion about what was meant by 'Inner Cities' led to the introduction by the Churches of the more accurate designation of 'Urban Priority Areas': most people living in these (twice as many as in the Inner City and predominantly white) are to be found on the perimeter estates. These lie just outside the half wheel we have described, and in a similar pattern across the river. The largest number of those in 'acute deprivation' and 'long-term unemployment' live on these outer estates.

As far as the Inner City is concerned there have been near-tribal differences between 'North End' people (again predominantly white) and 'South End' people, who include most of Liverpool's black community. These Inner-City areas are where the population has declined most: they include pockets of very severe deprivation and unemployment.

The population of the whole city of Liverpool at 400,000 is now half what it once was, though Merseyside at 1.4 million has a population not much short of Northern Ireland. The two cities of which we still have to provide the tale, are not separated by the River Mersey. The division is social and economic, affecting employment, housing, health, education, transport, services of all kinds, building up to that global phrase, quality of life.

The Liverpool Quality of Life Survey, undertaken by the City Council's Chief Executive's Department in 1989, accepted the same definition of poverty as used in the television programme of that time called *Breadline Britain*. This went beyond the question of being able to afford the minimum necessary for survival or subsistence. It defined poverty as the inability to afford a way of life that most people in society at that time considered to be the minimum acceptable. To be unable to afford three or more socially determined necessities was to live in poverty. To be unable to afford seven or more such necessities meant cutting back in all areas of life and experiencing a life of intense poverty. Applying these definitions to Liverpool, the Quality of Life Survey found that 40 per cent of Liverpool's population (or 41 per cent of all households) lived in poverty, and 15 per cent of the population (or 16 per cent of all households) lived in intense poverty. The 1990 *Breadline Britain* survey found that 21 per cent of the British population lived in poverty and 7 per cent lived in intense poverty. Thus these figures suggest that the levels of poverty and intense poverty in Liverpool were about twice the equivalent national levels.

What were these basic necessities used as a measure of the poverty line? There were some twenty-two socially perceived necessities listed. These included for Liverpool 47 per cent unable to afford a week's annual holiday, 23 per cent not being able to afford a damp-free home, and 34 per cent having had to forgo essential heating at times during the previous year. Examples of particularly vulnerable groups included the unemployed (72 per cent in poverty, and 26 per cent in intense poverty), lone adult families (68 per cent in poverty, and 31 per cent in intense poverty) and Council tenants (68 per cent in poverty, and 32 per cent in intense poverty). Finally the Survey showed that although the incidence of poverty occurred throughout Liverpool, it was far more prevalent in some areas than in others. The Report tells us that in the poorest area of the City ('consisting of four inner city wards and two outer estate wards') six out of ten households lived in poverty, and three in intense poverty. This compared with less than two out of ten households living in poverty in the most affluent wards of the City (cf. *Liverpool Quality of Life Survey*, City of Liverpool Chief Executive's Department, 1989).

It is true that this particular Survey – containing the latest details available – was made as the recession was striking the nation's economy. But the 1991 Census figures continue to show unemployment as slightly over twice the national average. There is little reason to believe that the same is no longer true of the poverty rate with which it is clearly closely linked. In the early years of the Thatcher Government, when the slimming down of industry was emphasised in the name of competitiveness, there were warnings that the rich would grow richer and the poor poorer. Our tale of two cities has confirmed this.

The Liverpool City Centre plan of 9 December 1993 claims that 'topographically, the City Centre lies in a shallow basin. On the land [east] side it rises to a ridge of low hills on which are sited the two cathedrals. On the other side is the shore of the Mersey with its long line of docks and warehouses, punctuated by the dramatic Pier Head group of buildings. The business and commercial core lies at the centre of the basin around a small depression once filled by the old Liver Pool.' Not surprisingly the Plan goes on to emphasise the importance to be attached to enhancing the City Centre's role in the local community to secure the regeneration of the city and Merseyside in general. To cope with competition elsewhere in the North West and to respond to future opportunities on the continent of Europe, there is need for continued private-sector investment to back up public-sector funds.

This calls for the partnership of which we wrote in the previous chapter. Already it has established, working alongside the Merseyside Development Corporation, an astonishing degree of restoration, regeneration, rejuvenation and new use for much of the City Centre. This has been an important feature in the attraction of tourism and leisure interest in an area rich in architecture and maritime concern. Its maintenance will be a great challenge to the future and will make a hefty demand on available funds and grants. There had to be attention to this part of what we used to call the 'hole in the heart' city. It must be kept healthy if the well-being is to spread to the extremities of the body. But the planners must be careful lest the concentration of resources at the centre should leave little to be expended on the areas of deprivation at the perimeter. This balance has to be assessed with particular care over the expenditure of the Objective One status money from Europe. It promises far, far larger sums than City Challenge (£600 million over six years), though this is not overwhelmingly great when divided between five Districts. On the one side of the scales must be put the importance of using it for investment which will produce jobs, rather than for subsidy which ends after six years: on the other goes the need for effective change to be seen in the poorest areas. After all Objective One status has been awarded to Merseyside because the Region is poor in European terms. The needs of Enterprise City must not be met totally at the expense of Hurt City.

Visitors to Liverpool speak rightly, though with surprise because of the image from afar, of the quite spectacular regeneration in the City Centre. Some of it has had the effect of reducing or removing altogether housing which served those employed in offices and occupations which no longer exist. We have welcomed the efforts made in recent years to be sensitive to the somewhat battered communities which have sometimes hung on in deplorable buildings in order to stay together rather than be scattered through being rehoused in different parts of the city. The classic example is that of the Eldonian Community, of whose efforts to stay together and create their own riverside village we wrote at some length in *Better Together*. They seem to go from strength to strength, with additional facilities such as their home for elderly residents and their own 'village hall'. It was a real celebration of co-operative effort when their leader, Tony McGann, was awarded the MBE and subsequently an honorary degree in Liverpool University. The headlined reminder that he was formerly an unemployed fork-lift driver in a local factory said much for the resilience of Liverpool people and their creative capacity given the opportunity and the knowhow of how to make a start.

A more recent example has been that of St Andrew's Gardens, formerly the 'Bull-ring' – as this circular tenement block has been termed. There, in the past, community life had been intense. Solidly built in brick and concrete, it had housed over two hundred families, but the massive five-storeyed building had gradually fallen into decay. Gradually, its accommodation was condemned as unfit for habitation. But this had to be set against the fact that the Bullring was a listed building and could not be demolished. Very much under protest, families were moved elsewhere in the city, sometimes to estates where conditions were not always much better. When at last it had reached the stage that about a hundred families remained but refused to move because they did not wish to be separated, they appealed to us for help. Through the good offices of the Merseyside Task Force we eventually secured a visit from the Minister for Housing, Sir George Young.

DEREK WORLOCK: I had the privilege of taking the minister into the Bull-ring where a representative group of the residents had been gathered. With great agility he followed them upstairs and down and along the endless balconies. Then he addressed them with remarkable patience and understanding. They could not be expected to live there in the future. The whole place would have to be refurbished and would provide student accommodation for the two Universities nearby. Meantime new housing would be built in the adjoining streets and they would all be offered accommodation there. They were a bit suspicious at first: they had received many promises in the past. 'No,' said Sir George, 'the money is promised. All I need to know is the sort of housing you want: bungalows, maisonnettes, semi-detached, or what?' The reply came from their most eloquent spokeswoman: 'It doesn't matter what it is so long as we can stay together. You see, we're a community here.' The Minister understood well, though it was unfortunate that when they asked him when it would all start, he replied that he had all the money ready and that the starting date would be 1 April. At last they got over that, and only a year or so later the building of new houses began. Many of those residents were there recently when I went to open the first houses and hand over the keys to the new occupants. It was a wet but very worthwhile occasion.

DAVID SHEPPARD: Another example of a project which had a small beginning more than ten years ago has now become a 'flagship' of Liverpool's City Challenge. It shows what can happen as a result of partnership between public, private and voluntary sectors, making the most of public money where people are ready to seize good opportunities. This is the Women's Technology Project, which has offered quality training to give women the skills needed to find their way into jobs with reasonable prospects. The new development will bring increased resources to training women over twenty-five, especially from Liverpool 7 and 8, who have missed out on school qualifications. We first visited the project soon after the riots when it was housed in temporary offices in Hope Street. Then it moved over to the Trade Union Unemployed Centre. Now Blackburne House is being refurbished to provide for the expansion which is taking place. A high proportion of the most hopeful developments in Urban Priority Areas are led by women.

Government ministers were surprised that Liverpool was the first city to embrace a Housing Action Trust (HAT). The seventy-two high-rise blocks in the city were given the opportunity to vote whether to accept this government project: it meant moving in the short term, and perhaps in the long term, away from management by the Council to Housing Association or private management. All but four blocks voted in favour. Housing Co-operatives have pressed ahead, though more slowly as less public money was made available. The very obvious needs of homelessness in London have highlighted the need for resources there. The housing needs of Merseyside are rather different: a huge catching-up operation is needed due to the poor state of repair of the housing stock. While modest private-sector building for sale helps, there is a very great need for decent housing at affordable rent.

In 1992 new offices and workshop spaces for small companies in developments such as the Brunswick Business Park attracted more than four hundred new companies and created four thousand new jobs in the teeth of the cold wind of recession. For the first time in ten years this meant a net gain of jobs (1,300). Merseyside has seen the birth of many small businesses, but in the course of several years, deaths of businesses have outnumbered births.

The year 1992 was also the best year yet for 'levering in' private-sector investment to support the public capital in the MDC's projects. These are more often than not modest 'green shoots', but together they reveal a steady increase in confidence. Project Rosemary, inspired by Derrick Walters, Dean of the Anglican Cathedral, is a £60 million development, backed by public and private money, bringing a new hospital, a factory, housing for students, and local Housing Association developments. It will mean in the long term a modest number of high-quality jobs in the heart of Liverpool 7 and 8. The experience of Liverpool University as a large local employer nearby, still employing comparatively few local people at anything above the most menial tasks, is a reminder that providing jobs in the right place is only half the battle. Careful monitoring and appropriate training are needed if local people, especially local black people, are to obtain good jobs.

There seems little doubt that generally speaking there has been a modest growth in confidence that Liverpool can be an Enterprise City where a good living can be made. The Port of Liverpool has re-established itself as the busiest on the west side of Britain. In 1983 it took 4,000 men to handle 8 million tonnes: in 1992 400 dock workers landed a record 27 million tonnes. In the same year Ford at Halewood won the award for the highest quality control of any Ford plant in the world: no mean achievement, especially when one recalls the deprecating tones with which the former Prime Minister used to speak of 'Hale*wood*'. Tourism also has grown with the £44 million restoration of the Albert Dock, with the Tate Gallery and Maritime Museum added to the city museums and art galleries, the Royal Liverpool Philharmonic Society, the theatres and, not least, our two Cathedrals. Tourism now directly provides employment for 1,400 people and generates £40 million per year. Despite the difficulty in securing national publicity, the Tall Ships Race finishing in the River Mersey in 1992 produced from its one week a net profit of £18 million.

Chris Farrow, Chief Executive of the Merseyside Development Corporation, who arrived here from the London Docklands Development in 1991, has written: 'When I spoke to people in London who had worked in Liverpool, their attitude tended more to the managed decline of Merseyside. Then Michael Heseltine began to press for a revival. I do not believe that regeneration is yet entirely secured, but there are enough positive assets to secure not just regeneration, but to turn Merseyside into an economic powerhouse for the North West and for the nation.'

It is of course easy with hindsight to speak of the need for a consistent strategy and long-term policy. We have already mentioned the rapid turnover of ministers with responsibility for most aspects of

Merseyside life and its economy. In industry and commerce evaluation of company activities rightly criticises short-termism, with its failure to attend to long-term investment in training, research and development. Short-termism affects government policies too, as ministers come and go. Sticking to consistent policies for ten years at a time might well achieve more in turning around the 150-year-deep decay of an old city than by three-year projects stacked up one after another.

In our democratic system, Governments, Local Councils and Councillors all have to give some sort of account of themselves at the ballot-box. The temptation for people with responsibility to look for quick returns to establish their reputation is considerable. Nationally each minister must seek to make his mark in a distinctive, personalised way. The same temptation exists at the local level. A leading councillor remarked in the 1970s, 'We don't want policies in this city. They get in the way of wheeler-dealing.' Then all of us learn to play the game of proving that our needs are the greatest. The late Alfred Stocks, a most distinguished Chief Executive of Liverpool (and the first Speaker of MARCEA), used to say that he was like a man standing on a beach with a surf-board. He would look out for a good wave which would give Liverpool a run, and then try to ride on it with his surf-board. Competitions with prizes awarded by government ministers accentuate the risk of replacing regular policies by projects. In recent years Liverpool has done quite well, when grants have been available for enterprising *ad hoc* initiatives. We have seen one new set of urban projects stacked up on top of the other, sometimes displacing the other before its benefits have been established. It will be interesting to see whether the newly proposed Single Regeneration Budget produces more consistent policies.

Government programmes which aim at regenerating the City Centre almost inevitably affect those in the perimeter estates least of all. 'Trickle down' does not reach them: nor does 'ripple out'. It must be remembered that in Merseyside twice as many people live in the perimeter estates as are to be found in the Inner City. For example, the Borough of Knowsley comprises largely Urban Priority Areas, built to house inner-city people from Liverpool at a time when fashionable policies led planners to shift people from old overcrowded cities out to green-field sites. But mass unemployment is two or three generations deep in parts of Knowsley such as Kirkby and Huyton, on estates which are themselves not much older. Some 41 per cent of children in Knowsley are growing up in a home where no adult is in paid employment. It has also to be remembered that these perimeter estates have less of the resources which historically voluntary bodies have offered in the old inner city. For example, more than 70 per cent of salaried youth work in Liverpool runs under the banner of one voluntary body or another and 30 per cent comes under the statutory bodies. In the Borough of Knowsley, the percentages are almost exactly reversed.

When the perimeter estates were built, the local authority funded most of the youth work. The effect of the subsequent cutbacks has been even more devastating.

The most effective government programmes involving perimeter estates have been carefully targeted at points of need and not left to chance or charity. Appointed as Minister for Merseyside following the Toxteth riots, Michael Heseltine was shocked by what he saw in one particular perimeter estate: he had asked Jim Lloyd, the leader of Knowsley Council, what was his biggest problem. He replied, 'Cantril Farm'. When the minister visited the Estate two days later he saw in his words 'A disaster which looked beyond retrieving.' His pathfinding approach was driven by pressure for dramatic action. The transformation of Cantril Farm to Stockbridge Village was the largest of all the Heseltine initiatives. It was reviewed in 1993 by Richard Evans and Hilary Russell (*Stockbridge Village – Achievements and Lessons after 10 Years*, European Institute for Urban Affairs, Liverpool John Moores University, 1993).

Knowsley District Council sold the estate to Stockbridge Village Trust in an 'untried recipe' for Public/Private partnership. Barclays Bank, Abbey National and Barratts were partners with Knowsley, supported by major injections of public money from the Department of the Environment. The review commissioned a survey by MORI of 10 per cent of households. The response showed residents highly satisfied with the Trust's achievements: 80 per cent thought that the estate had improved over the last ten years, and was now a good place to live. When asked which body they wanted to be responsible for their homes, 77 per cent opted for the Trust or the Village Housing Association; only 5 per cent nominated the Local Council. Some 25 per cent of dwellings were now owner-occupied, largely through Right to Buy.

Before the Trust took over, tenants had been using every possible method to have themselves rehoused outside Cantril Farm. The population, planned for 18,500 never reached more than 14,000. The 1991 census, probably underestimating numbers, recorded 6,362. On 31 January 1993 there was a waiting list of 799 names seeking housing in Stockbridge Village, the majority from outside the estate.

Repairs have been tackled more promptly; major alterations have been made to improve security. The top floors have been taken off the high-rise blocks, security phones have been installed, terraces of houses have been reversed to ensure that neighbours face neighbours, and porches have been added. Cul-de-sacs have been created, to block off roads which gave vandals easy escape routes. All this is the result of listening to what people say they want: a true sense of security is near the top of the priorities on large urban estates.

The fear of darkness, of debt collectors, dogs, burglars and vandals, has to be allayed or overcome before responsible community life can develop. The fear of young fire-raisers has also been real – one primary school was burned down for the second time. Attempts to rebuild it were on two further occasions frustrated by more fires. Eventually a specially constructed building was completed, with metal casements, high protective fencing and floodlighting. For the opening the achievement of rebuilding was reminiscent of a police barracks in Northern Ireland. But the floodlit building soon became a show-piece for residents and visitors alike. This costly act of perseverance and commitment has survived, although the architect and builders claim only that it is vandal-resistant, not vandal-proof, lest this be put to the test.

The 'untried recipe' has provided a model from which Housing Action Trusts (HATs) and Large Scale Voluntary Transfers have learned. It has been a remarkable achievement. At the same time Richard Evans and Hilary Russell reflect,

> Problems remain despite the evident relief of housing distress. A number of indicators – unemployment, car ownership, single-parent households, eligibility for free school meals, clothing grants and housing benefit – show that the Estate's socio-economic standing relative to the rest of Knowsley has remained constant or even declined. This situation points not to any failure on the Trust's part but, if anything, to the narrowness of its terms of reference. It puts a question mark against an urban renewal strategy based solely on housing.

We sometimes hear reports that 'millions have been poured' into some project. It is difficult to evaluate such expenditure until one can examine comparative figures. When the Meadowell Estate in Newcastle erupted in riots a few years ago, it was alleged by a broadsheet newspaper that £1 million had been poured into that estate only the previous year. If that meant something like £100 per head of the residents, it was not necessarily very generous: more of a splash than a 'pouring in'. At a cautious estimate £27 million of public money, together with major contributions from the Private Sector, was injected into Stockbridge Village. This was for a project which, as we have seen, was confined to housing needs. It demonstrates the scale of help needed to turn around a 'hard to let' estate. It is worth remembering that, when he was out of office, Michael Heseltine made a series of speeches in which he said that to reverse the decline, the old cities required resources far beyond the capacity of the private sector alone.

Private-sector investment is nevertheless often the yardstick by which bids for public monies are measured. City Challenge is an attempt to put a substantial public grant where it would attract private-sector investment. The big prize is £7.5 million a year for five years for each urban area that wins the competition. It is a considerable incentive, though it can be a severe blow to the morale of those whose bids are unsuccessful. City Challenge is not fresh money for urban initiatives. It is 'top sliced' from Urban Programme grants allocated to Programme authorities. But a variation of the poverty trap can often operate. Knowsley, which comes top on most league tables of need, took the bidding for City Challenge very seriously. There was a high level of community participation in the preparation of the bid. There was also a huge sense of letdown when it became known that Knowsley was not among the winners. To add insult to injury, the Borough's Urban Programme money was sliced away to provide the City Challenge prize money for the winners. There can be little doubt that by the yardstick of the award going to those places where needs were shown to be greatest, Knowsley should have won. But a major factor in reaching the decision was how much private-sector investment would be attracted. Yet the absence of private-sector involvement is already a factor in creating the poorest areas. Liverpool's first bid for part of the City Centre attracted a number of private investors, anxious to see the regeneration of that area carried through. But its second bid for the perimeter estate of Speke and neighbouring Garston failed, for the same reason as in Knowsley.

The strategy is quite understandable. Decisive progress can be achieved in chosen areas, often with knock-on fringe benefits, but our concern for the whole shouts loudly that the needs of the poorest perimeter estates grow more acute each time the major programmes go elsewhere. This is a Christian and apostolic concern for the weaker members of the body and for those who find themselves excluded from the good opportunities which are available to others.

In 1991 we became involved with another section of the community whose members can often find themselves the victims of disadvantage at a time when they feel increasingly powerless: those whose circumstances lead them to feel overtaken by old age rather than having achieved it. Thank God, a growing number of pensioners have found economic independence: 50 per cent of pensioners in Britain now own their own home outright. However, those who do not have occupational pensions can face a sudden and dramatic fall in income when they retire, along with the loss of the fellowship and sense of purpose of the workplace. All these sections of the community were represented when that autumn we delivered one of our four-part addresses to a great rally of pensioners in the Philharmonic Hall, half-way between our Cathedrals. The pensioners mustered there after marching through the city, and there was immense solidarity among them in firmly asserting their rights. We spoke strongly in support of the Pensioners' Charter, calling for pensions which would equal half the national average of earnings. This would do much for their personal sense of dignity. The independence resulting from this redistribution of wealth would enable pensioners to continue their contribution to the whole body, instead of fearing lest they be regarded as a burdensome liability for the rest of the nation.

Nowadays there is of course more than one generation in retirement and in receipt of a pension. Earlier retirement and better health care have brought about the so-called 'Third Age' of vigorous, healthy retired people. Many of them have a major contribution to make, as 'carers' for the 'Fourth Age' of more dependent elderly people, and in support of the 'Second Age' in which the difficult skills of parenting call for the wisdom of years. The Church is learning slowly to recognise the skills of 'Third Age' people and to invite their active participation in the life of both Church and community, instead of allowing such skills and wisdom to go to waste. But in the Fourth Age there are revealed some quite unacceptable inequalities. Too much emphasis on setting proprietors free from red tape, so as to run their retirement-home business more profitably, can carry some severe risks. There must be no relaxation of inspection, if neglect, exploitation and abuse are to be avoided.

Looking at this matter in still greater depth, it is reckoned that there are some six million voluntary carers serving old people at home. This is estimated to save the nation some £24 billion each year. The carers themselves need help at times from support services, not least in the provision of periods of respite. This emphasis on better support services is also included in the Pensioners' Charter. Provision of health care affects not only the elderly, but everyone. The 'health map' of Britain, and indeed of Liverpool, shows serious inequalities in taking up health care.

DAVID SHEPPARD: When I was invited to give the Dimbleby Lecture in 1984, I spoke of 'The Other Britain' and instanced some of the inequalities in health provision. This proved a sensitive subject where some people were concerned. An angry letter from the then chairman of the Liverpool Health Authority denied strongly that there were any inequalities in the health provision in Liverpool. All the recent publications on Liverpool's health have shown that ill health appears with dramatic clarity in the poorer districts on any health map. The health divide is not only between Liverpool and more affluent regions, as the 'Quality of Life Survey' [referred to earlier in this chapter] showed, but also within Liverpool itself.

By contrast with the defensive comments of the Liverpool Chairman, a doctor in the North East of England recognised that the take-up of health care in his general practice was far below the national average. He told me that his reaction to the Dimbleby Lecture was to take on additional lay staff, so that it was possible to reach into more people's homes with education about the promotion of health. A few years later he published figures in the British Medical Journal, *showing that the local take-up of health care was now above the national average* (cf. G. N. Marsh, *Efficient Care in General Practice,* Oxford University Press, 1991).

From what we saw together when visiting townships in South Africa in 1989, there are many benefits to be gained if doctors are able to train local members of the community as health assistants. We were impressed not only by the valuable help these people could render but also by the acceptance of such assistants by the community from which they had been drawn. It has seemed to us wasteful that in high-unemployment areas in Britain local people should be unable to participate in health education. They would bring the great advantage of understanding the culture, the ideas and the fears of their neighbourhood better than many of the professionals, who are in any case few on the ground. Only occasionally in inner-city primary schools has one stumbled on a group of young mothers being trained for such a purpose as this by the local medical officer or school nurse. This could be extended.

In our reference to the 'Quality of Life' Survey, we have shown the apparent connection between poverty and ill health. Even though the clinical details are not always clear, unemployment is without doubt a serious factor in ill health and early death. Dr Richard Smith wrote in *The British Medical Journal* (October 1992), 'Unemployment raises the chance that a man will die, and for those in middle age – with the biggest commitments – that chance doubles . . . Exactly how unemployment kills is unclear, but it is through a combination of poverty, stress, adoption of unhealthy behaviour, and the devastating effect on mental health.' In its Report for 1991 the Liverpool Health Authority reviews the evidence given in *Liverpool: Healthy City 2000*, and claims that a socially and economic productive life for all Liverpool people would make the greatest contribution to equity in health.

Much of that kind of change depends on decisions made far away from Liverpool. Meanwhile, the Health Services realise that the quality of Primary Health Care will do more to shift the so-called 'health divide' than any high-profile and high-budget argument about hospital treatments. The Liverpool Family Health Services Authority has in fact made steady progress in providing better health centres where primary health care can be more accessible. In the summer of 1993, at the request of the Health Services Authority, we cut the first sod for an expanded Health Centre in Toxteth. It will be right in the heart of the local community, and will have close links with the University and the Teaching Hospital. This should encourage some of the ablest students to see for themselves the importance of General Practice work, instead of its being the poor relation of specialisms with their high-publicity advances in treatment.

DEREK WORLOCK: Developments of this kind cannot come too soon. Watching the sod-cutting exercise that morning was a young man with a child in a pram. I congratulated him when he told me he lived nearby. He would benefit greatly from the future Centre, I told him. He hung his head and said that he was leaving the district shortly. There were too many jobless youths around and his home had been broken into three times in the previous month. Then typically he added that perhaps he would move back one day, provided there was a job going.

Between the floorboards of poverty we keep noticing the lurking dry rot of unemployment. We have already referred to the 'two times factor' – twice the national average for both the poverty rate and for unemployment – and we have just noted the connection between poverty, unemployment and ill health. From the most utilitarian point of view, mass unemployment costs a nation far too much in Benefits; but when people are excluded from paid work for long periods, their value to the community is itself diminished. Unemployment isolates you from the mainstream life of the nation, prevents you from making your contribution to the common good and takes away self-respect and the sense of being valued.

There is little doubt that the sense of being caught in the poverty trap was heightened by the introduction of the Social Fund in 1988. The National Audit Office's calculations were that the Social Fund's arrangements were successful in achieving the Government's economic objective of saving money. But it questioned whether the Fund was offering effective help to the poorest. Discretionary grants were never over-generous, but the cuts brought about by the Social Fund regulations were drastic. For most applicants the change meant loans rather than grants. Many of the poor have a horror of the money-lender and of loans. Yet soon the indebtedness to the Social Fund included multiple loans. In any case the facility varied greatly, in accord with whether the local office had money left in its annual quota. In some years a quarter of the applicants were turned down for that reason, even though nationally millions of pounds remain unspent each year.

Amid such fears, many additional demands have fallen on voluntary and Church sources of relief. our clergy tell us that they have never had so many requests for help at the door. The picture is lightened by occasional reports of the establishment of Credit Unions, though often financial help and experience are needed to get such initiatives off the mark. On the darker side our Salvation Army colleague told us of food being stolen from their store for the first time in his experience. The

Furniture Resource Centre was established in South Liverpool, initially with substantial grants from the Church Urban Fund. It collects gifts of furniture and delivers to the poorest households, often referred to it by Merseyside Social Services.

The resources of the poor, their families and the charities which have endeavoured to help have become more and more stretched as years have gone by and distress has increased. The Chairman of the Furniture Resource Centre wrote to us: 'If a society is in any sense to be judged by how it treats the poor, the disabled and the powerless, then the operation of the Social Fund is an indictment of an uncaring society.' Yet recently the Cabinet minister, Michael Portillo, has tried to argue that a Christian insight into current cutbacks must agree to reducing levels of benefit so that, for example, parents would take more responsibility for their children. He claims that Christian ethics are not about taxation and state intervention, but instead call for individuals to take responsibility for themselves and, through charity, for the needs of other people. We have consistently claimed that such an argument falsely sets up opposites. We strongly believe and preach the personal responsibility of individuals. At the same time we emphasise that New Testament Christianity is not about individuals standing on their own two feet. It is also about being members one of another, about bearing one another's burdens.

We believe that it is right to evaluate policies in the light of God's concern for the whole body and especially for its weakest members. Indirect taxation, like VAT on necessities, means that all pay tax regardless of their income, except where some goods are zero rated for those on benefit. This scarcely accords with Christian insights about levels of giving within the body of the Church. St Paul told the Corinthians that they were to give in proportion to their means (cf. 2 Corinthians 8). Taxation is a way in which as citizens we express our belonging to the body politic. Progressive income tax asks people to pay in proportion to their means. The steady move away from such direct and principled taxation to indirect taxation on necessities falls as a heavy blow on the poor. The reluctance to pay direct taxes was played on in the 1970s and 1980s by the repeated use of the catchphrase about things being at the expense of 'the tax-payers' money'. Christians might have reminded people that when Jesus was asked about paying taxes, he spoke of giving back to Caesar what was Caesar's, not the tax-payers'. When in recent years the nationalised industries were being sold off, it was claimed that they were being given back to the people. No one would answer the question of where the money raised was used for the community, save in the reduction of taxes for the upper wage-brackets.

Christians have been taught over the years to speak of themselves as the stewards of the gifts God gives us, not the outright owners. Taxation is a way in which we make our contribution to the whole. It was our clear impression, when the Report *Faith in the City* was published, that many people all over the country expressed their willingness to pay more in taxation to produce better opportunities for the poor.

When we came to Merseyside in the mid-1970s, we soon had to learn that unemployment here was not cyclical but chronic. Our experience has made us sceptical of claims that full employment will or can be brought back by any of the policies currently displayed on the political shelves. What we have seen in Merseyside is the tip of an iceberg which has steadily become more visible across the industrial world. In 1994 the European Community has some 19 million unemployed, half of whom are long-term unemployed (i.e. for more than twelve months).

Where the City of Liverpool is concerned, we have fairly detailed figures for unemployment, as supplied by the 1971, 1981, and 1991 Censuses. For Liverpool the unemployed of working age are given as 28,666 in 1971, 46,812 in 1981, and 41,129 in 1991. In case that may suggest a slight fall at the time of the third census, the unemployment rate for the three counts (i.e. the number unemployed of working age as a percentage of the economically active population of working age) was 10.6 per cent in 1971, 20.4 per cent in 1981, and 21.6 per cent in 1991. A further division shows that in 1991 the male unemployment rate was 26 per cent, compared with the female rate of 15 per cent. Perhaps of even greater significance, especially when analysis is required for Objective One status, is the undoubted fact that over the two decades between these three censuses the City experienced a sustained decline in employment. During that period the number of jobs in Liverpool decreased by nearly 40 per cent, at a time when there has been a 0.7 per cent increase in employment for Great Britain as a whole.

Statistics are soon outdated. They provide a snapshot, though over a period they can indicate a trend. The figures we have quoted cover a twenty-year period and provide an example of the 'twice times' factor: twice the national average. But for job losses over that period the proportion is much higher. No doubt much of this has been related to the introduction of advancing technology into industry and administration. The reduction in job opportunities is likewise reflected in the population fall. If, as we believe, that last figure is finally evening out, there is little sign as yet that the distinction between the Two Cities has lessened significantly. The distinction will present a real 'two cities' challenge to the opportunities which seem to be opening up as a result of the grant of Objective One status.

Meantime the Major Government apologises for having had to raise taxation beyond what it had forecast at the last General Election. The Opposition parties taunt the Government by alleging that the new and increased taxes are being raised to pay for the mismanagement of unemployment. The Social Justice Commission, chaired by Sir Gordon

Borrie, declared recently that there cannot be a healthy economy in a sickly society: 'Poverty in the midst of plenty is not only morally unpleasant, but also extremely expensive. It has been calculated that every high school "drop-out" in the United States costs the country $300,000 over their lives in lost earnings, increased likelihood of crime and the like . . . Indeed, because the great majority pay the costs of unemployment, crime and ill-health, making the poor poorer makes us all poorer too' (*Social Justice in a Changing World*, Institute for Public Policy Research, 1993, pp. 13, 22).

Some commentators have now borrowed an objectionable word from across the Atlantic and refer to such people as we have described – the poor, the long-term unemployed, the victims of the Social Fund – as the 'underclass'. Often the thrust of using that term is to claim that poor people belong to this 'underclass' because of some incapacity or laziness in themselves. Such an analysis may indeed be described as 'massaging' statistics, because it allows portrayal of the prosperity of a city or nation, while ignoring the poverty of a sizeable number of its citizens. This was done when the city-states of ancient Greece prided themselves on their democracy. Slaves and women had no part in that democracy. They did not count. Talk of an underclass runs the risk of making similar dismissive judgments – hence our 'tale of two cities'.

The years ahead will undoubtedly call for painstaking study of the nature of work and the future of employment. Changes in society have already raised the issue of full employment and its alternative, if all are to have the opportunity to achieve the dignity of human labour and enough money to live on. A theology of work starts, as we indicated in the previous chapter (p. 33), with God the Father of all, the Creator and Sustainer of the universe. Charged with breaking the Sabbath laws, Jesus said, 'My Father continues to work, and I must work too' (John 5:17, REB). Human beings are called to be co-creators, fellow-sustainers with our Creator and Sustainer God. The Protestant Work Ethic took a wrong turning with far-reaching effects when it lost its original sense of the 'Calling', or vocation to work; for this had something transcendent about it. The worker was called by, and must answer to God who cares about the whole of his creation. When the Caller was forgotten, the work ethic took an individualistic turning. Wealth creation became increasingly about money, for me and mine. The calling or vocation had been to develop the wealth of the universe as God's good stewards, and to see that it was distributed for the good of the whole. Developing the wealth of the universe must include the development of people and not their waste.

We do not try to claim that all work can feel creative. Dirty, dangerous, exhausting work in mines or docks has enabled men to experience the sense of solidarity in a workforce, and to hold their heads up high. It was not simply the pay that made them feel needed;

nor was it this which enabled them to believe that they were playing a vital part in the economy. Yet pay was important if the worker was to feel valued. Nowadays vast pay differentials have developed to say what individuals are worth in the market, and these can deny human values when placed in the context of the whole of life. There are of course many examples of the value of voluntary or unpaid activity in the service of the community. This too can be creative and sustaining work. We regularly meet mothers, carers, voluntary and church workers who feel a great sense of obligation to the people they serve. Do such callings depend on some old echoes from traditions and understanding about commitment for God's sake, or for the sake of neighbours? We think they do. Such a response is put to the test in today's consumer society, where values generally are equated with pay and power. The skill and enterprise of many in commerce and industry deserve good rewards. Improvements in health care, education, social services and conditions in urban priority areas depend on a sound economy, as we have seen in this chapter. But our judgment would have to be that unacceptably high disparities have widened in Britain, and between our 'two cities'.

Nor can we forget what Pope John Paul wrote in his Encyclical Letter *Laborem Exercens* (1981) on Human Work:

> In spite of all this toil – perhaps, in a sense, because of it – work is a good thing for man. It is not only good in the sense that it is useful or something to enjoy; it is also good as being something worthy, that is to say, something that corresponds to man's dignity, that expresses this dignity and increases it. If one wishes to define more clearly the ethical meaning of work, it is this truth that one must keep particularly in mind. Work is a good thing for man – a good thing for his humanity – because through work man not only transforms nature, adapting it to his own needs, but he also achieves fulfilment as a human being and indeed becomes 'more a human being' (Article 9).

'The Liverpool Three. In one sense ... the most significant development of all' (Introduction). John Newton joins us in dedicating the chapel at the new Marie Curie Centre in Woolton.

The service to launch the Council of Churches for Britain and Ireland was held in Liverpool. All the four nations' Church leaders were there, led by Archbishop Runcie and Cardinal Hume.

'There are still a few contemporary ancestors, who haven't heard that peace has broken out' (Chapter 1).

'The enormous crowd singing and walking along Hope Street' towards the
Metropolitan Cathedral (Chapter 1).

The three MARCEA Presidents, with the Rev Bob Andrews, the full-time Ecumenical Officer, who serves all our churches (Chapter 1).

Christmas carols in the shopping precinct. *'The City Centre is certainly the hub of the Merseyside region'* (Chapter 3).

The Eldonian Community create their own riverside village. Tony McGann, Paula Ridley and John Moores help us cut the first sod for their village hall (Chapter 3).

The Borough of Knowsley, comprising largely urban priority areas, claims that its refuse collection is highly cost effective. We learn how.

Looking at some of the *inequalities in the health provision in Liverpool* (Chapter 3). With Protasia Torkington at the launch of her book.

Flying off to one of our joint visits to Northern Ireland. This was a January flight for the week of Prayer for Christian Unity in Armagh and Belfast Cathedrals (Chapter 4).

Remembrance Day in Liverpool with Rabbi Malcolm Malits. *'God has given us many universes of faith, but only one world in which we live together'* (Chapter 4).

In South Africa *'we were repeatedly impressed by the gracious and resilient black people we met and by the quality of leadership, often given by women'* (Chapter 5).

We visit Archbishop Desmond Tutu at Bishopscourt, Cape Town. *'The remarkable feature of the Church in South Africa is that its realism is lit by a certain joyful hope'* (Chapter 5).

Grace Sheppard and Julian Filochowski, Director of CAFOD, accompanied us on our three-week visit to South Africa (Chapter 5).

We arrive to dedicate the joint church at Cinnamon Brow, Warrington New Town. *'Moving towards shared witness would contribute significantly to the Mission of the Church, and allow the light of the Gospel to shine more fully on the moral perplexities in today's world'* (Chapter 6).

Being there at times of tragedy and disaster (Chapter 6). Archbishop George Carey visits Warrington following the explosion of an IRA bomb in the busy shopping precinct.

A service at Anfield Football Ground brings to an end the two weeks of mourning after the Hillsborough disaster (Chapter 6).

Grace Sheppard receives an Honorary Fellowship at Liverpool Polytechnic, now Liverpool John Moores University. In a previous year we had been made Doctors of Technology, on account of our bridge-building. Derek presented Grace for her Fellowship, having heard that morning that he had lung cancer (Chapter 6).

4

Sharing Our Faith

At the approach of the 1990s, the Anglican Church, together with most Protestant Churches, made a world-wide commitment to finish this century with a Decade of Evangelism. At much the same time, though on a separate occasion, Pope John Paul called on Roman Catholics to commit themselves to a Decade of Evangelisation. Our critics were quick to suggest that we could not even agree on a shared title for what many had welcomed as a combined initiative. Who had got it wrong? Our experience was that the words are not interchangeable. Each reflects different insights, if not priorities. Once again there was much to be learned from this, provided the approach was of openness rather than contention.

We take 'Evangelisation' to mean living and speaking and working in such a way that the light of the gospel is shed upon every aspect of life. It is a broad word, broader perhaps than what many Christians identify as 'mission'. It encompasses 'Evangelism' together with all that God sends us to be and to do in his world. In this chapter we shall place our focus on Evangelism, which we take to mean naming the name of Christ, and we shall write of Evangelisation and shedding the light of the Gospel on today's world, in Chapter 5. We hope in this way to deal positively with two complementary aspects of the Christian faith we share, rather than just sort out what for some seemed to be a frustrating and confusing distinction.

To us Evangelism means 'naming the name of Christ', implying a personal conversion of heart (whether that happens abruptly or out of long Christian nurture) and the challenge to discipleship in the communion of the Church. The Decade of Evangelism was clearly a call to decision and to the deepening and sharing of personal faith; but prolonged over a ten-year period it inevitably meant facing the challenge of how that faith has to be sustained and proclaimed in society as it is at the end of this millennium. That challenge made great demands and we were genuinely surprised that in many parts of our region the Decade went off with a bigger bang than we had expected. Brightly coloured posters proclaiming that 'Jesus is Lord' abounded and were not altogether a surprise; but the launch of the Decade seemed to give people the courage and incentive to declare their Christian commitment.

In some parts of the country it is suggested that the Decade has become stuck, or that it failed to get off the ground. This may have been due to complacency rather than acute or hurtful differences of belief and practice. In other parts of Britain, though, extended prayer and planning seem to be leading gradually to effective programmes through which the faith is shared. With John Newton for the Free Churches, we issued a joint letter to be read in all the Churches and communities in Merseyside. We suggested a three-phased process in which (i) we should start by looking at ourselves and our knowledge of Christ and his gospel; (ii) in light of that shared knowledge, we should look at our relationship with one another; and (iii) we should try to see how we could jointly convey the truths of the Gospel to the world.

In the first stage, Roman Catholics were encouraged to read right through one Gospel, that of St Mark, and a number of ecumenical study groups profitably took this to heart. The centre of attention in the second stage has in many cases been the Eucharist, which has often meant that the focus has been on a point of painful division. Where more recently attention has turned to the broader concept of 'communion', then it has not stopped at relationships within our own Church, but has included ecumenical partners and how sharing the faith with others can become a reality in the neighbourhood. Even so, few understand how the imperfect or partial communion, which describes the relationship between our Churches, is an obstacle to our sharing Holy Communion or eucharistic hospitality. It remains a major challenge, especially in Churches where it is seen only as a question about approaching the Lord's table. For an increased knowledge of Christ and commitment to his teaching inevitably leads many to desire to share in the central point of worship. We shall return to this subject in the final chapter.

Where the straight challenge of evangelism is concerned, some fear that an attempt to proclaim the gospel ecumenically must almost inevitably blunt the message. In fact the Decade should encourage Christians of different traditions to be bold and clear about what our Lord Jesus Christ means to his followers. We do not wish to smooth over our distinctive witness, but we believe that there are many occasions when our witness is stronger and more credible if we are seen to proclaim it together.

A fair example of this was when John Newton and the two of us delivered a three-part address in St Helens. More than forty local churches are committed together to the Decade in a process called St Helens Inter-Neighbourhood Evangelisation (SHINE). They invited us to speak at an open-air service in the town-centre precinct: it was the climax of a week's witness based on a marquee set up there for the purpose. We planned our address together, using the reading they had chosen for us from Isaiah 58. The first would proclaim the Kingdom of God and its values; the second would treat of the call to unity and faithfulness in the Church; and the third would deal with the call to discipleship. An extract from each of the three parts may provide an example of how our joint testimony may add to rather than blur the Scriptural message.

DAVID SHEPPARD: When we read the Gospels, especially Matthew, Mark and Luke, we find the central teaching of Jesus is about the Kingdom of God. He does not immediately say, 'Follow me' when he meets people. By an action or a story he says, 'The Kingdom of God is like this', 'This is my Father's purpose for how the world should be', 'This is what I stand for'. When people have grasped something of his plan, then he says to them, 'Follow me. Join the people of God in the Church who will work together for my Kingdom in the World.'

In Isaiah 58 we are called to be restorers of houses in ruins. This means not just in our church life, but in our family life, so that we can call young people to the adventure of chastity, of faithful, life-long relationships: to restore houses in ruins in our community and public life, so that the needs of the poor and unemployed are not pushed to the margins: to restore houses in ruins in business life, trade unions, in the professions, in education, in law enforcement, so that justice and truth can be relied on: in international affairs so that the poorest countries are given much better resources and trading conditions from countries like ours.

JOHN NEWTON: The Church, as the servant of the Kingdom, should be the place where the Kingdom way of life shines out most clearly. I hope that SHINE may help to bring Christians in St Helens into still deeper unity in Christ, so that the world may believe. Personal witness is important but the Church, to be an effective sign, must be united, bringing into that unity those who have become estranged from the community.

The Church must also be loving. For love turns the focus of the Church outward, from self-concern to the outgoing love and concern of Christ for all people. This can be given expression by those engaged in SHINE, as they go into neighbourhoods, streets, homes, in prayer and caring concern.

Finally, the Church must be missionary, sharing the good news of Jesus Christ with all who will hear. John Wesley's great phrase in regard to the evangelising work of the Christians was 'I offered

Christ': not just 'do-gooding' or preaching the social gospel, but the outflow of the love of Christ which constrains us.

In all this we shall be doing the deeds of the kingdom, Christianising society, ministering to the poor, the needy, the disadvantaged, in Christ's name. Today that means the unemployed, the lonely, the drug addicts, AIDS sufferers, the terminally ill. This is the world to which we are called to proclaim the gospel of reconciliation.

DEREK WORLOCK: I am asked to focus on 'discipleship' but in any case I would have settled on that lovely verse about 'a watered garden, like a spring of water, whose waters never fail'(Isaiah 58:11). For me it is special, not so much because of the River Mersey, but because I was brought up in a peaceful Hampshire village where the clear waters of the chalk-streamed River Itchen flowed below, and occasionally watered, our garden. And as a child it fascinated me to think of the source from which each individual droplet of water came to join, as it were, the torrent of grace which moved towards the ocean, keeping our land fertile. You do not have to be a countryman to see what I am getting at: the source of our faith which enlivens and inspires us is our Almighty God himself, infinite, eternal, the Creator, who made us and all about us. And 'discipleship' is all about following the maker's instructions, living them, sharing them.

Let us be clear that the call is not to part-time discipleship: something that we just switch on for a few hours each week, when we have done our work, fulfilled our responsibilities at home, and are free to take up the work of the Gospel as a self-chosen hobby. The call to discipleship is a call to a way of life: at home, at church, at work, in every breath we breathe, in all our relationships, in what we are as well as what we do.

When we ask ourselves how in practice we expect to share our faith with people in a largely unchurched, multi-cultural, multi-faith, pluralist country, we know that we face a gap whose width cannot be exaggerated. No clear-flowing chalk stream, it is like a great river. There need to be great stepping-stones, and rafts on which our neighbours can avoid being swept away and can perhaps detect the light of the Gospel, before many of them are likely to say, 'This Christ could be for me.' Sometimes evangelism can seem to them like a challenge to leap for the banks of a strange and unknown shore. For them courage would be the means of receiving God's grace, rather than openness to truth and faith. Trust can be a preliminary to the discovery of faith, not just its consequence.

William Abraham's widely acclaimed book *The Logic of Evangelism*

(Hodder & Stoughton/Eerdmans, 1989) insists that true evangelism must mean initiation into the Kingdom of God, with its concerns for justice and truth throughout the whole of God's world. It is sometimes said that Evangelism is the primary task of the Church. But we cannot accept that. When Christians make Evangelism the sun around which all other Church activities must circle like planets, our motives become seriously distorted: for example, we do not offer service to the needy so that we may evangelise them, but because the Lord we profess asks us to show such concern in response to his love. The same distortion takes place if growth in membership and property is made the primary task of the Church, as though the institution as such existed for its own sake.

The first priority for the Church is worship. This is where our Christian character is formed. Learning to worship together helps to give us a shared calling from the Lord who loves the whole world. We do not have to take Christ into the world. He is already there, sometimes inspiring the process of change, sometimes wounded by developments which trample on human worth. He calls us to join him in working for his reign in the world, in building up his Father's Kingdom. With his help and with many allies we are called to change the course of events, adding a new dimension to a world which often does not know him. When we say that the Church is in, not of, but for the world, it does not mean that we must adopt the ways of the world. Nor in reaction to worldliness should our prime or sole concern be with Church affairs. It is a denial of the call to Evangelism to restrict our contacts and concern to the 'converted'.

For many people, young or old, the first point of interest will seldom if ever be with what they see as 'churchy' matters. It is more likely to be when the Church is seen attempting to serve hungry, homeless, unemployed or oppressed people, or engaging with integrity in complex contemporary issues, or celebrating in some way the life of the local community. There is of course the danger that those in the first stages of enquiry may assume that the Church is simply involved in social 'do-gooding'. They will not easily make that mistake for long if they stay around with us for a while. Our motivation springs from the love of God which we experience through Christ. His suffering, death and resurrection, and the outpouring of the Holy Spirit upon God's people, is at the heart of the good news. Evangelism includes explaining what Christ has done for us, and this has to be in terms which others can understand. God's way of salvation is not just a piece of common sense: it is good news for people who need, and sometimes almost unconsciously seek, forgiveness and the inner strength to live the way they believe to be right.

Some Christians still assume that the traditions of our Churches are in total disagreement about the content of the Gospel. The second Anglican–Roman Catholic International Commission (ARCIC II) tackled the old battlegrounds of justification, faith and good works in its Report entitled *Salvation and the Church* (Church House Publishing and Catholic Truth Society, 1987):

> Above all it was agreed that the act of God in bringing salvation to the human race and summoning individuals into a community to serve him is due solely to the mercy and grace of God, mediated and manifested through Jesus Christ in his ministry, atoning death and rising again. It was also not a matter of dispute that God's grace evokes an authentic human response of faith . . . The difficulties arose in explaining how divine grace related to human response.

For both of us discipleship means a living, daily experience of that undeserved love of Christ, and a confidence that beyond this life he will take us to the Father: exactly how he will do it, we do not know, but we are prepared to trust. That trust or faith is itself a gift of the God we strive to follow and through word and example to exemplify to those we serve. It is not always easy to be a sign of good news. There are many times when in this too we are able to be of help to one another: for instance, a phone call to express support when a journalist has done a hatchet job on the other. But often the encouragement and indeed God's word come to us from the sickbed of those we visit in our pastoral round.

Both of us have known those visits when we have found the sick person dying 'in sure and certain hope'. That great lay Christian worker, Patrick Keegan, endeavoured in his final weeks to focus his mind entirely on the Lord he had come to love, so that visitors to his bedside had almost to engage in a three-way conversation. He sent messages of encouragement and thanks to his friends but always with the assurance of his love of Christ. It was as though Jesus was already in his room with him and he wanted to hear nothing which might distract him from that fact. Yet others, who have lived hopeful and faithful lives, can suffer acute depression or dementia in extreme old age. That is part of the infirmity of the body and does not take away from the secure reality that 'underneath are the everlasting arms', nor from the promise that in the Kingdom of God there will be an end to death and to mourning, to tears and to pain. St John makes it clear that no one will be excluded because of blameless ignorance; only because of deliberate, conscious rejection of truth, love and the opportunity for repentance. 'This is the judgment: that the light has come into the world, but people loved darkness rather than light because their deeds were evil' (John 3:19).

John Newton has borrowed for the title of his recent book (*Heart Speaks to Heart*, Darton, Longman and Todd, 1994) words chosen by Cardinal Newman for his motto, and used by Archbishop Michael Ramsey at the first British Faith and Order Conference in 1964: 'In a depth below doctrinal thought and structure, heart speaks to heart.' That does not mean that we are indifferent to doctrinal thought and structure. It does mean that we recognise Christian brothers and sisters from the other side of dividing lines which some have thought were required by loyalty to be made permanent walls.

A few years ago the three of us had a memorable experience of heart speaking to heart. We were stranded on a foggy Sunday night in Belfast. No planes were taking off. We had been together to Armagh for the installation as Archbishop of Cahal Daly, who as a Bishop in Belfast had met with us on many occasions in the 'North-West Triangle' group of Church leaders. That night the three of us stayed together in a hotel, which subsequently suffered severe damage in an arson attack; we even found time late that evening to prepare material for some future joint engagements.

Next morning it was still dark as we waited for a taxi to the airport. When at last it arrived, the taxi driver examined us and our luggage carefully before he started to drive us. After some minutes he started to tell us why he had looked so carefully at our bags. 'You can't be too careful these days,' he said. He told us how some ten days before, he had answered a call from a fare who sat at the back of the taxi, carrying a large parcel. Soon our driver felt cold metal pressing into the back of his neck. He was ordered to deliver the parcel to a certain public address, and was warned what would happen to him if he failed to do so. 'It's amazing how much of your past life crowds into your mind at such a time,' he told us. In fact he managed to leave the parcel in a place where the damage was limited and no one was hurt.

He went on to describe how his wife took him to the Chapel with her the following Sunday. Then he told us very simply of his conversion which had followed. He spoke with love and courage of his new-found confidence in God's protection. It was not that he was fearless. He longed for peace and an end to violence, but now he could face each new day with trust in God's love for him.

We were well wrapped up in overcoats and scarves, so nothing seemed unnatural when he asked David, who was sitting in the front, if he was a Christian. David replied that he was and added, 'Look, you're not going to believe this, but I am a Bishop of the Church of England, and in the back of your taxi you have a Roman Catholic Archbishop and a Methodist Chairman.' Our driver took all that in his stride: he nodded a 'God bless you' through his driving mirror, but evidently the news about his passengers was as nothing to the surprise he had sustained the previous Sunday when the Lord had revealed his love for him in the local Chapel. At the airport we wished each other peace and Godspeed. As we walked to the plane, Derek Worlock said, 'I think I understand now why God allowed our plane to be cancelled last night, though I am not quite sure which of us needed that encounter most.'

On another of our joint visits to Belfast, a senior Presbyterian minister spoke to us of a member of his congregation who used to tell him very critically that he did not preach the Gospel. One day she asked him, 'Did you hear that woman this morning on the radio? She was *really* preaching the Gospel.' 'Yes, as a matter of fact I did,' he replied, adding, 'Did you notice who she was?' 'No, I missed the announcement.' 'She was a Roman Catholic.' 'Well,' she said, 'you can't trust anybody these days!'

The life, death and resurrection of Jesus Christ and the pouring out of the Holy Spirit must always be at the heart of apostolic preaching. These were the mighty acts of God, the *kerygma*, the essential gospel which the apostles proclaimed. Some Christians have assumed that, in order to be absolutely faithful, we must always make precisely the same proclamation in exactly the same terms at all times and in all places. Yet a more careful look at the Acts of the Apostles makes it plain that the apostles took full note of the distinct cultures they met. They began where people were, endeavouring in this way to achieve the greatest understanding of the gospel message.

When the apostles preached to Jews, they could assume common ground in understanding that there was a good and purposeful Creator God. So they spoke from the beginning about the mighty acts of God in Christ, events which had happened in their midst. When they spoke to Gentiles they could not assume that common ground. The Acts contains two speeches addressed to Gentile audiences. One comprised the dialect-speaking inhabitants of an agricultural area in Lystra. The other was made up of the intellectuals of the cultural centre of the world, Athens. In both these situations Paul's preaching of the Gospel centres on a good and purposeful Creator. He speaks of a God who shows kindness, sends rain for the crops, gives food and good cheer. This was full of meaning for rural people: it was within their experience. Paul also met the Athenians on their own ground, finding meeting points wherever he could with the Epicurean and Stoic philosophers whose writings they knew.

We both listened to a very moving address on Evangelism and Culture at the annual Northern Church Leaders Consultation. It was in 1980 when we were approaching the Nationwide Initiative on Evangelism. The speaker was David Brown, Anglican Bishop of Guildford, who died in office two years later. He told us that he was called to be an evangelist before he was called to be a priest. He served first in southern Sudan, where through his own preaching he saw thousands of people respond to the Gospel and go on to be baptised.

He moved north from there into the Muslim world to do some research work in Khartoum and Amman Universities. There he saw no conversions, no baptisms: 'it was the same gospel, the same Churches involved, Roman Catholic and Protestant, the same devotion, the same methods, the same Bible, the same sacraments, the same preacher'. But the response was entirely different. He drew our attention to the sharply differing cultures within which he was serving. In southern Sudan people were coming out of Animism: the Church had a dynamic internal partnership with the culture that was being created – involved in establishing education, health care, economic growth.

In the Muslim world the Church and its preachers were trying to win people from a proud and long-established culture to something alien to their mould of thinking. He went on to say that, if we were to evangelise people of other faiths, we must talk about God first, the good and purposeful creator God: 'The whole problem in Islamic missionary work is that we never tell the story in such a way that a Muslim can hear it. And we don't do so because we haven't worked hard enough at it, and we aren't humble enough to become part of that culture. We stand on our own bases of truth, as if other people hadn't got any truth.'

DAVID SHEPPARD: I found myself identifying with much of David Brown's experience. It's not that I have worked in a Muslim culture. The two cultures I compared from my experience were both part of British life. I came to personal faith at Cambridge University: that was the environment in which my faith grew up until ordination. Then, after a curacy, I was plunged into the East End of London, Canning Town. There were six regular communicants when I first went to the Mayflower Family Centre. It was not part of the local culture to think of Church-going as a serious adult proposition. Breaking fresh ground was a long, hard struggle throughout the twelve years we were there, though there was a steady trickle of new Christians. At intervals during those years I went back to Cambridge to preach. Always there was a substantial response: many people there seemed eager to embark on the Christian journey. Like David Brown, I had the personal experience of a dramatically different response, even though the Gospel was being preached by the same preacher.

DEREK WORLOCK: Some years ago, a Times Magazine *reporter came to interview me for an article in a series on the childhood of people subsequently prominent in some sphere of life. He questioned me about my parents and my early home life. When he learned that I had always felt called to be a priest, he said, 'But that's terrible. No turning point, change of direction, incident leading to conversion?' I had to disappoint him, though I was ready to talk of changed circumstances in later life. He was not interested. But the changes in the culture amid which I had exercised my priestly ministry have been immense. Westminster, Stepney and Portsmouth in the South, and then transferred without warning to Liverpool in the North. The North/South Divide, as it was called, provided a sharp contrast in circumstances and social conditions. But the change in cultural attitudes in each part of the country affected relationships and values, and often called for radically different pastoral techniques with which to present the unchanging Gospel.*

When the Anglican report *Faith in the City* was published in 1985, we both saw the recommendation to parishes to hold a Mission Audit as an effective way of helping the local Church to look outward. It was a challenge to listen to the local culture, whether it was sophisticated and secularised, or feeling shut out from the Church as from other institutions. We both felt able to commend mission audit programmes, rewritten in more appropriate language for Liverpool parishes. The word 'audit' in the title raised some misunderstanding and apprehension in both our dioceses. The title was changed to 'Mission Assessment Programme', but for some the association with audits remained a block. It seemed to put the focus on their parish finance, whereas their sacramental and other programmes stressed spiritual values and at the same time the generous use of talents, time and professional skills. It had to be spelt out clearly that the listing and sharing of such talents and the willingness to serve would form part of the parish survey which was being attempted. A Mission Assessment does not look just at the size of the local Church membership, but at the wider community it is called upon to serve. What are its strengths? What are its needs? Are there recognisable groups who do not come to Church at all? What beliefs do they hold, and what do they think about the Church? The answers invariably present a great challenge about our faith and what we share. It also shows often how our two communities can be a source of mutual reinvigoration.

The response from parishes embarking on this Mission Assessment Programme was very slow so much so that five years on we were asking if the idea was appropriate for our area after all. We were advised that we should persevere, and the Decade of Evangelism/Evangelisation brought fresh momentum. More than fifty parishes have now tackled a Mission Assessment Programme, and many of these have done it in ecumenical partnership with neighbouring Churches.

DEREK WORLOCK: I spoke on this issue of bridging the gap between the Gospel and Contemporary Culture in an address to an Ecumenical Conference at Swanwick in 1992:
'How do we tell our people in a way which is convincing and with real meaning about the Christ who guides our lives? How do we help them to see his relevance to their lives, even though they have not consciously, or at least formally, accepted possession of a Christian faith? In today's consumerist, get-rich society, or at least

hang-on- to-what-you've-got society, how can we or they make sense of the Beatitudes, which Christ set out as the way to true happiness?

'We do not serve the cause of truth by being hesitant or over-sensitive. My impression is that young people today welcome plain speech. They dislike being patronised, but expect us to start from an understanding of their position and of things which rank in their priorities.

'The underlying word, as it was with the mission of Christ and given by him to his disciples, has to be "love". It is easy to say that the word is overworked, and certainly contemporary culture will have much to do with how it is expressed. But love is generous, it does not dominate, it perseveres, and it has regard for the needs of the object of that love. If love is removed from evangelisation, the latter is reduced to emotionless canvassing: if it is a question of feeding in Christian truth without clear personal commitment, it does not have much likelihood of surviving to outweigh all the competing theories and ways of life.'

We wrote in *Better Together* about the importance of 'Being there'. Many of our neighbours will only begin to feel that Christ 'could be for them' when they see that Christians are present in the places where people are hurting. We will go on being there if we are genuinely interested in them, not as potential scalps for an evangelistic belt, but out of love and caring.

DAVID SHEPPARD: We can only express admiration for the way in which so many of our clergy sustain that presence in every kind of district. Often they take the strain at great personal cost. What is certainly a healthy emphasis on lay calling sometimes turns out to make clergy feel they are not regarded as so special. There are particular periods when they may feel beleaguered or insecure, such as 1994's financial pressures facing the Church of England. Some clergy flinch from putting the need for a substantial increase in giving to their congregations, when it seems that most of the money is for stipends. Sometimes the feelings of being beleaguered can be more literal: one spoke recently of the need to lock the vicarage door, which he had always resisted, and of needing to walk nightly round Church and Church Hall to protect the buildings from vandalism by groups of youngsters hanging around near the adjacent bus stop. That can be immensely wearing.

We salute too the clergyman who 'hangs in there' in a housing estate parish, where there is little tangible response. He refuses to give up, though he is frustrated by the difficulty of expanding occasional contacts with young people into real stepping stones, lacking, he feels, lay leaders with whom he can share that demanding reaching out.

We understand the conflict another feels in a parish with quite a large congregation. He says, 'It is more than delegating, but rather developing the inner team of leaders and giving the time that such development demands.' He feels the conflict between giving the considerable time such support takes and wanting himself to be in the front line of evangelism in meeting people outside the Church community.

Sometimes the emotional and spiritual cost is plain: it can bring spiritual growth, as in one case, where the sensitivity and learning through struggle are a strength which the altogether self-confident do not know. Where some have to find creative ways of living a single life, for those Anglican clergy who are married there are added tensions over the division of time to be resolved: typically of many, one married priest feels the conflict between family space and the constant demands of the local neighbourhood.

'Living communion', of which we often speak nowadays, means that Christians live out the implications of our worship in relation to other Christians and to every neighbour whom God draws across our paths. 'Towards Koinonia in Faith, Life and Witness' was the theme of the 1993 Fifth Faith and Order Conference of the World Council of Churches. It met for the first time for thirty years in Santiago de Compostela; Faith and Order includes the Roman Catholic Church and Pentecostal communities who are not members of the World Council of Churches. At this Conference, the Orthodox Metropolitan of Pergamon, John Zizioulas, delivered a major paper on 'The Church as Communion': 'When we say the Church is Koinonia, we mean no other kind of communion but the very personal communion of the Father, the Son and the Spirit. It implies also that the Church is by definition incompatible with individualism: her fabric is communion and personal relatedness.'

St Paul used to speak of the Church of God of a certain place: Corinth, Philippi. 'There is no Church which can be conceived in herself, but only in relation to something else – to God and to a certain locality, i.e. to the world around her,' said Metropolitan John. In the Lima Report, *Baptism, Eucharist, and Ministry*, it is emphasised in the same way that our eucharistic celebrations always contain the call to mission: the Eucharist is truly understood as 'precious food for missionaries'.

There is a famous passage in Pope Paul VI's Apostolic Exhortation on Evangelisation in the Modern World (*Evangelii Nuntiandi*, 1975), which spells out what 'Living Communion' can mean:

Take a Christian or a handful of Christians who, in the midst of their own community, show their capacity for understanding and acceptance, their sharing of life and destiny with other people, their solidarity with all for whatever is noble and good. Let us suppose that in addition they radiate in an altogether simple and unaffected way their faith in values which go beyond current values, and their hope in something that is not seen, and that one would not dare to imagine. Through this wordless witness these Christians stir up irresistible questions in the hearts of those who see how they live.

DEREK WORLOCK: Pope Paul VI's Exhortation Evangelii Nuntiandi *was written in response to the 1974 Synod of Bishops on 'Evangelisation in the Modern World'. It proved to be a momentous effort on the part of the Church to face the challenge of giving Christian witness in the different cultures existing in today's world. We began to hear for the first time that word 'indigenisation', soon to be replaced by 'inculturation'; and we had to face up to the problem of how to present the face of Christ in a multi-racial society, with its different cultures according to the stage of development of the nation and continent concerned.*

At the height of the debate, a West African Bishop spoke strongly of the problem presented to his people by some Western outlooks and disciplines, and by customs suited to Rome and the frozen north, but quite inappropriate to his people in West Africa. He was strongly attacked by the German Bishop of Berlin, who pleaded for total uniformity, adding that any deviation in such matters in his divided diocese would have left them prey to communists and atheists and opponents of the Church. Whatever the culture, the members of the Church must be totally one and orthodox, conforming in every way with Peter in Rome. The reply of the African was memorable and to a great extent unanswerable: 'I wish to assure His Excellency,' he said, 'that I too believe fully in the teachings of the Holy, Roman, Catholic and Apostolic Church. All I ask is to be allowed to live these teachings as an African.'

Among the neighbours whom God draws across our path are also people of other faiths. Living in communion with Christians does not exclude respect for other people's faith journeys and histories. The Dominican theologian Jean Tillard, writing after the Faith and Order Conference in Spain (*The Tablet*, 4 September 1993), says that such respect breeds mutual trust, making possible real collaboration. 'This is true not only for questions concerning peace, justice and ecology, but also – and, it seems to me, mainly – for the crucial dialogue with the other religions.' Archbishop Robert Runcie, addressing the Inter-Faith Network, said it was imperative that the Christian churches, at the same time as engaging in the Decade of Evangelism, should think through 'the place of other religious traditions in our account of truth'.

The announcement of a Decade of Evangelism in a country like Britain was almost inevitably seen as a threat by some minority groups who hold other faiths. It is hard for those of us who belong to the majority community to understand how real such a threat can feel. We have no doubt that at the present time the greatest threat to all faiths comes from secularism; but many Jews understandably fear that what they see as proselytising by Christians may take away young people, on whom the future survival of Judaism depends.

DAVID SHEPPARD: A small group of Christians and Jews to which I belong was shown a video: it was produced, no doubt with some selectivity and defensiveness, by a Jewish body, in order to expose what they regarded as aggressive Christian evangelism. It showed Jewish students being targeted at moments when they might be expected to be especially lonely and vulnerable. The Head Teacher of the King David High School in Liverpool told us that he had shown it to his sixth formers. Because of its nature, he arranged separate showings for Jews and Gentiles. The Gentile group was appalled, upset, wondering how their Jewish friends would react; they expected them to be very angry. In the event, the reaction of the Jewish group was a surprise to them. The attitude of several was characterised by fear and withdrawal; some said that they probably would not seek a university place after all.

If we are not to target Jews, what do we make of a text like that in St John, where Jesus says, 'No one comes to the Father but by me'? We believe that Jesus Christ in an altogether unique way is the Saviour of the world. We believe that his death on the Cross made 'the atoning sacrifice for our sins, and not for ours only but also for the sins of the whole world' (1 John 2:2). The mystery of that atonement is beyond tidy theories: it is beyond time, effective for all the human race.

St Paul's model of the justified believer is Abraham, who had never heard the gospel about Jesus, but had put his trust in the promises of God which were known to him. Paul writes of those who have not heard the Christian gospel in chapter 2 of his Letter to the Romans: 'They show that what the law requires is written on their hearts, to which their own conscience also bears witness; and their conflicting thoughts will accuse or perhaps excuse them on the day when, according to my Gospel, God, through Jesus Christ, will judge the secret thoughts of all' (Romans 2:15, 16). This is not to patronise or even colonise them by claiming them to be 'latent Christians'. It does allow us to believe that there may be many Abrahams living by faith. who belong to other religious communities. William Abraham writes of a 'high Christology', which extends the effect of Christ's sacrifice through all time and all creation: this 'creates space for openness and generosity to other religious traditions'.

The reason why we should share the Gospel of Jesus Christ is not because we believe that all those who have not heard it are on the road to hell: it is because the Lord himself asks us to do it. It is part of the response we make to his love. In our approach to those of other faiths we shall rightly enter into dialogue, based on deep respect for the other person and for their faith journey. Whatever the background of the other person, we must avoid manipulation or exploitation of power and influence. Respect for others includes being willing to share our precious beliefs, as well as listening with genuine attention to what is precious in their beliefs to those others. In loving dialogue a Christian will not be hesitant about explaining what Christ means to him or to her. But our repentance from the terrible treatment Christians have meted out to Jews down the centuries, including our own, should include renouncing deliberate and aggressive targeting of Jewish people for evangelism.

Nearly thirty years have passed since the Second Vatican Council issued its Declaration on the relation of the Church to non-Christian religions. The Declaration included these words:

> Since Christians and Jews have such a common spiritual heritage, this Council wishes to encourage and further mutual understanding and appreciation. This can be obtained, especially, by way of biblical and theological enquiry and through friendly discussions. Even though the Jewish authorities and those who followed their lead pressed for the death of Christ (cf. John 19:6), neither all Jews indiscriminately at that time, nor Jews today, can be blamed for what happened in the passion of Christ. Consequently, all must take care lest in catechizing or preaching the Word of God, they teach anything which is not in accord with the truth of the Gospel message and the spirit of Christ. Indeed the Church condemns every form of persecution against whomsoever it may be directed. Remembering, then, her common heritage with the Jews, she deplores all hatreds, persecutions, displays of antisemitism levelled at any time or from any source against the Jews (*Nostra Aetate*, n.4).

In some sense, that Declaration – though a breakthrough for many at that time – still speaks with the language of the mid-1960s. Recently, at the time of a top-level ecumenical gathering in Jerusalem, a member of the Rabbinate was reported as saying, 'We are the generation called upon to love God more and to stress religious differences less.' These words apply to Christians as well: they do not imply indifference to truth.

We live in a pluralist society. Does that then mean that there can be no shared, common morality? Or that we must end up with some lowest common denominator, searching for a universal world religion? The Chief Rabbi, Jonathan Sacks, insists that we need to learn two 'languages' – a public language of common citizenship and the language of our own faith community. Unless we cherish the deep spiritual roots of our own faith, we shall not bring the tang of our distinct flavour to the chunky stew of a multi-faith, multi-cultural society. By contrast, the melting pot, which assimilates all our faiths into some inoffensive well-wishing hotch-potch, melts down the distinctive riches of religious traditions into a misleading indifferentism in which all truth is obscured.

Christian evangelism in a pluralist society calls people to believe, to be baptised, to become disciples, to belong to a community in which we may find meaning, vision and a moral language. These are the treasures which we bring into dialogue with other faith communities and with the whole community of nation and world. But, this is very far from a strong and intolerant fundamentalism which insists that God has given one totally clear revelation, in such manner that anything else must be rebutted, and all other religious traditions must be forced into line. Such an attitude sees tolerance as something soft-centred and feeble, the weakness of the wimp. In another age G.K. Chesterton, famous for his paradoxes, said that tolerance was 'the virtue of people who do not believe anything'. We have both been criticised with the charge that in the name of tolerance we have lacked conviction in standing up for our own particular tradition. That is not how *we* see it.

We believe that there can be a strong spirit of tolerance, built on the secure foundation of revealed truth and on the experience of the living God in today's world. Alongside that affirmation we would place Jonathan Sacks's claim that tolerance 'is the virtue of those who believe unconditionally that rights attach to the individual as God's creation, regardless of the route he or she chooses to salvation. That is, the belief that God has given us many universes of faith, but only one world in which we live together' (Jonathan Sacks, *The Persistence of Faith*, Weidenfeld & Nicolson, 1991). In a world containing Bosnia, Rwanda, Israel, Iran, Iraq and Northern Ireland, tolerance should rank high among the theological virtues.

We do indeed need to learn those two languages, suggested by the Chief Rabbi – a public language of common citizenship and morality, and the language of our own faith community. At the same time, as part of our Christian evangelism, we respect and listen to the languages of other faith communities. If we are to let the light of the Gospel shine on the life of the whole world, we need to deepen our knowledge of the Gospel and to understand the culture and traditions of all other believers.

Pope Paul VI held together the witness of life and lip in his Exhortation on Evangelisation in the Modern World:

There is no true evangelization if the name, the teaching, the life, the promises, the Kingdom, the mystery of Jesus of Nazareth, the

Son of God, are not proclaimed . . . This proclamation – *kerygma*, preaching or catechesis – occupies such an important place that it has often become synonymous with it: and yet it is only one aspect of evangelization . . . Evangelization is a complex process, made up of varied elements: the renewal of humanity, witness, explicit proclamation, inner adherence, entry into the community, acceptance of signs, apostolic initiative. These elements may appear to be contradictory, indeed mutually exclusive. In fact they are complementary and mutually enriching. Each one must always be seen in relation with the others (*Evangelii Nuntiandi*, 1975, Articles 22, 24).

5

'To the Ends of the Earth'

In their sermons when administering confirmation, all bishops speak often about Pentecost and about the mission given to the disciples by the risen Christ before his ascension into heaven. For he promised them that they would receive the power of the Holy Spirit and were to be his 'witnesses in Jerusalem, in all Judea and Samaria, and to the ends of the earth' (Acts 1:8). Even with today's most up-to-date technological communications, the task entrusted to the disciples was humanly speaking impossible. From those transformed but frightened men, it called for faith and courage and the power of the Holy Spirit. It is not surprising that today's evangelists find the mission equally daunting. Doubtless the apostles were upheld by their memories and personal knowledge of the Lord who had called them. Today's evangelists have to deepen that same personal knowledge and devotion if their motivation is to surmount the secular pressures of contemporary society.

It is not just a matter of language and of distance. We can read what happened when the disciples proclaimed the word to the polyglot crowds on the morning of that first Pentecost: 'we hear them preaching in our own language about the marvels of God' (Acts 2:11). There was also, and still is, the problem of helping the hearers to understand the unthinkable, to believe the humanly incredible, and to recognise the message of the Gospel today as the good news of salvation, with a unique relevance to the life of each one of them. As we wrote in the previous chapter, the culture of those to whom witness is to be given is a major concern; and culture is much more than intellectual attainment.

DEREK WORLOCK: I remember explaining at that 1992 Swanwick Conference on Gospel and Contemporary Culture that the fundamental question they faced was how far gospel values, which are

77

accompanied us, together with Julian Filochowski, Director of CAFOD (Catholic Fund for Overseas Development). Early in our visit one of the Roman Catholic bishops replied to Derek Worlock's enquiry about Desmond Tutu: 'There are things which he says which I could not go along with, but the man is a prophet. If you are looking for the way ahead, it is he who will show it. You will find that he has both the anger and the joy of a true prophet: it even comes bubbling up in his worship.' We were soon to see this for ourselves, as we shared in worship with him and saw him meeting with his clergy and presiding over the Synod of the Church of the Province of Southern Africa.

During our stay we managed to visit or to stay overnight in a dozen black townships. Staying overnight was intended to provide an opportunity for people to approach us who might have been reluctant to do so under the gaze of some officials interested in our presence. We were very moved by the way in which we were trusted by the local black communities. It was clear to us that this trust was given to us because of the stand for justice and truth which Church Leaders had taken. At the end of our visit we were invited to Durban to address the Anglican Provincial Synod which meets every two years. It gave us the opportunity to play back, in a four-part address, some of the impressions we had formed.

DEREK WORLOCK: 'We salute the prophetic role of the Church – or must we say "Churches"? – in South Africa. In this we have special regard for the leaders of the Churches for their courageous, faithful stance. To be a faithful prophet is not easy, reluctant or not. The prophet points the way where to go and where not to go. Sometimes a prophet will be accused of making mistakes or using the wrong words. But the way he proclaims is the right way. His voice and his role are authentic. Not infrequently the prophet gives expression to a voice which otherwise is not heard. In Old Testament times the voice of the prophet was customarily of doom and gloom, usually with reason. The remarkable feature of the Church in South Africa is that its realism is lit by a certain joyful hope. Because it is the Church of Christ, that welcome note in your witness, characterised in a unique way by your Archbishop, must be right and a sign of confident hope for the future.'

DAVID SHEPPARD: 'We were repeatedly impressed by the gracious and resilient black people we met and by the quality of leadership, often given by women. In several places there was clear pride in the community and resentment that decisions about their lives were taken over the heads of the community, as though white people knew best. We were keenly aware of the waste of

God-given human talents, because black people are excluded from decision-making and from responsible positions.

'Some commentators, both here and in Britain, have told us that change is inevitable. When we hear them saying this, our minds go back to a man standing in the door of his shack in one of the townships. Surrounded by squalor and poverty, he raised his hands to heaven and asked us over and over again, "When and where? When and where?" Undoubtedly the stubborn ruthlessness of many who have power in South Africa today makes us exceedingly doubtful whether, simply through some kind of economic development, any fundamental change is inevitable. We feel bound to ask what measures may bring effective pressure to bear on the government which will achieve the fundamental changes required for the dismantling of apartheid.'

In those dark days, when so many political leaders were in prison, Church Leaders provided in effect the only voice for justice that could speak in public. But when the following year Nelson Mandela and the authentic leaders were released and able to take part again in public debate, the Church Leaders like Desmond Tutu pulled back from the very public stance which until that time they had adopted. In the long years of apartheid and of waiting there would have been a vacuum without them. Now their role lay more clearly in providing support, peace-making and reconciliation. We saw for ourselves the way in which those with whom responsibility now lay took courage from the experience and vision of long-time heroes like Archbishop Denis Hurley of Durban, who had stood unflinchingly against apartheid for forty years as a bishop.

The need for vision has always been an important part of the equipment of the prophet. We shall not understand what our Lord meant by his key phrase 'the Kingdom of God' unless we can look back to the prophets of the Old Testament, whom he often quoted. Walter Brueggemann says that the task of the prophetic imagination is to 'penetrate the numbness' (Walter Brueggemann, *The Prophetic Imagination*, Fortress Press, 1978). Many people are so numbed that they cannot imagine that this world could ever be different from what they themselves have known. They are numbed by their own limited opportunities, by anxiety about money, or by the bread and circuses of our day, which fill so much of the media. 'This numbness knows no future except more of the present. It cannot imagine a new gift. It is able to believe no more in the graciousness of God than in the judgment of God.' Such a numbness is often comforted by a privatised religion. But the teaching of Jesus is both about another world beyond this one, and about this world and all who dwell in it. 'Our voice,' wrote Brueggemann, 'needs to bring a transcendent dimension. When Moses and the prophets stated their belief that "the Lord will reign for ever", they were often adding under their breath "and not Pharaoh".' The present structures will not last for ever. We are on a journey through this world and beyond it. The more strongly we believe the promise that the Kingdom of God and its justice will come fully into being in a world beyond this one, the more our yearning hearts will find unbearable the contradictions to his rule which face us in today's world.

There are new considerations when we see ourselves as part of Europe. Through a European programme such as Objective One status, major benefit is due to come to Merseyside, alongside Northern Ireland and the Highlands and Islands of Scotland. Regions falling into poverty and historically isolated groups benefit from the generosity of the European Community. But the same generosity is not so evident towards more recent immigrants, where the poor of the Third World are concerned. Shedding the light of the Gospel on such public issues will include challenging the attitudes of 'Fortress Europe'. Even if not strictly xenophobia, it bears the mark and restrictions of a sort of continental isolationism. This attitude was epitomised by the Asylum Act, which passed through Parliament in 1992. As Chairman of the Church of England Board of Social Responsibility, David led an ecumenical delegation to the Home Office on three occasions. Concessions were made in Parliament on the important principle of an appeal for asylum seekers against the decision of immigration officials. Nevertheless the Act made tighter the restrictions preventing families from coming together.

The recent debate about the 'Back to Basics' policy turned sour when it became evident that the moral law applies to personal, individual and family life, as well as to attitudes and acts in social, economic and political life. In many, if not most, of these matters the teachings of our Churches are in agreement, though sometimes there is a difference in the language in which they are expressed. We welcome the growing tendency to see how our Churches can come together, not just for a combined call to prayer in a time of danger or crisis, but in the preparation and presentation of moral teaching and in combining to give witness when ethical issues are under scrutiny. A good example of this was the joint presentation of evidence to the House of Lords Select Committee on Euthanasia in 1993. Such combined witness was clearly influential in the Report subsequently issued. It can also be a safeguard against the attempts of some sections of the media to suggest division and to create conflict.

We have never disguised that there are certain issues about which we disagree. We regret those disagreements, but are ready to discuss them with one another. They need not present serious blocks in the way of the evangelising task which we share. In *Better Together*, we wrote at some length about our difference of belief about the ordination of women priests. It is still very much an issue, though we can both thank

God that our Churches are able to discuss together the consequences of the decision which the Church of England has taken. A number of very difficult issues have had to be approached, but, as Pope John Paul has said, 'without animosity'. He was echoing the sentiments of his predecessor, Paul VI, who wrote: 'Obstacles do not destroy mutual commitment to a search for reconciliation.'

To some onlookers it may seem that these differences are mostly about 'churchy' matters, about disciplines, traditions and new theological insights. Yet in practice some of the ethical issues of today touch very closely the personal life of individuals and communities. One such subject is that of the world's population growth and contraception. The media has attempted to set us against one another on this issue more than once, and especially at the time of the Earth Summit at Rio de Janeiro in 1992, when there took place the UN Conference on Environment and Development. Archbishop George Carey had visited the United Nations two weeks before the Summit and subsequently made use of some of the statistics he had been given. He said that the world population was expected to rise by 97 million every year until the end of the decade and then to double by the middle of the twenty-first century. He expressed surprise that apparently population control was not on the agenda for the Rio Conference, owing to 'religious issues'. He hoped to discuss the environmental crisis with the Pope when he made a private visit to the Vatican the following week.

This provided a field day for the media, and almost inevitably we were both drawn in. It is a good example of how we try to deal with an issue of public importance without our pretending to be fully in agreement, but also without being drawn into acrimonious and scandalous opposition.

DEREK WORLOCK: No one can deny that the continuing growth in the world's population has very serious implications for Third World development. It also poses a challenge to the world community generally for it is clearly related to the use of the world's resources and to global consequences for the environment. But it is not just a problem of demography. The numbers game by itself may startle, but merely to limit the number of births in the Third World is to be handing greater power to the 20 per cent of the world who live in industrial society over the 80 per cent who live in non-industrial society. The northern countries should try to solve the social problems created by poverty, lack of education and lack of health care rather than try to enforce control of population and families in the south by contraception. I believe in the concise formula that fewer people will be achieved by less poverty, not less poverty by fewer people.

DAVID SHEPPARD: I agree that the eradication of poverty comes first. Contraception would never provide a short cut to feeding the hungry world. The fears of people in the Third World that there will be no child to look after them in old age or to inherit their land are powerful motivations for having a large family. But there is no way in which the world will be able to feed the huge growth of population, if this continues with the improvement of health care. I believe that there is urgent need also for educational programmes which include easily understood ways of contraception. These can deliver women from the constant exhaustion of bearing large families, and set them free to develop their human potential.

This is an example of how the realities to which the eternal values of the Gospel must speak are constantly changing. Christians have to address questions which simply did not exist in a previous age. For me it is an expression of our trust in the living God to believe that he provides appropriate gifts to meet new needs. In this case, I believe that he enables scientific technology not only to deliver better health care, but to limit the increased population which results from it.

DEREK WORLOCK: The most important component of a population policy is the sort of basic development programmes which enable poor people at the grass roots to see that they have some control over their lives, and which will provide them with that level of security they need in times of crisis and old age. This is what in the West is called responsible parenthood, and can be largely achieved by natural family planning.

All the evidence is that wherever such sustained development has taken place, people choose for themselves to have fewer children. We have to be utterly opposed to coercion by the state or any other body, or to any other measures which subvert the free choice of the couple to exercise their right to have children. But the Church, through its medical and development agencies, must try to support legitimate efforts to help people understand responsible parenthood and to enable couples to make properly informed decisions about the number and spacing of their children. Of course this has to be done within the cultural and religious context of people's understanding of sexuality and the family. I still remember hearing Mother Teresa describing how her young Sisters were explaining natural family planning to a group of Indian mothers. Her verdict was, 'It was very beautiful.'

DAVID SHEPPARD: Anglicans and Roman Catholics agree that God calls married couples to responsible parenthood. We agree that marital intercourse should involve the two basic 'goods' of marriage, loving union and procreation. As Anglicans we believe that this intention should apply to the married relationship as a whole; whereas Roman Catholics hold that each and every act of sexual intercourse must be 'open to procreation'. They exclude the use of contraception, though 'methods of birth control based on self-observation and the use of infertile periods' conform to what they call 'the objective criteria of morality'. On the other hand the Lambeth Conference of Anglican Bishops in 1930 resolved that 'where there is a clearly felt moral obligation to limit or avoid parenthood, and where there is a moral sound reason for avoiding complete abstinence . . . other methods may be used'. Since then very many Christian couples have thoughtfully decided to use contraceptives with prayer to space and plan the size of their family.

DEREK WORLOCK: Pope Paul VI's letter Humanae Vitae (1968) was widely criticised at the time, but as years have gone by it is appreciated that in upholding the sanctity of human life he was condemning what has proved to be 'a contraceptive mentality'. There are now many former critics who have begun to appreciate the positive emphasis which he was placing on what are now called 'pro-life issues'. Nor should we forget what the same Pope wrote in his encyclical on human development, Populorum Progressio: 'It is for the parents to decide, with full knowledge of the matter, on the number of their children taking into account their responsibilities towards God, themselves, the children they have already brought into the world, and the community to which they belong. In all this they must follow the demands of their own conscience enlightened by God's law authentically interpreted.'

It is true that in presenting its teaching authoritatively, the Roman Catholic Church is often accused of being lacking in understanding and compassion. But in its teaching role, the Church gives no one service by selling people short where universal and unchanging moral norms, prohibiting what is evil, are concerned. Subjectivism can make chaos out of ethics. Circumstances can without doubt affect the degree of blameworthiness where an offence against morality is concerned. But they cannot change the objective truth of morality. There is genuine concern at the rise of individualism, which substitutes a privatised morality for the traditional insistence on moral absolutes of good and evil.

DAVID SHEPPARD: I agree that moral choices are not simply matters for private conscience. There is objective morality and we can know it. But even though the search for moral absolutes is understandable, it is by no means an easy matter to establish such absolutes. When it comes to particular situations, Christians often disagree about the conclusions to be drawn from a shared principle. For example, take the morality of waging war. We both sweated together over those questions about a just war again at the time of the Gulf War. All can agree about the commandment 'Thou shalt

*not kill'. Disagreements arise when the meaning of that teaching
has to be applied.*

*In the case of population control, I believe that we face a new set
of questions, different from the time when Christians first considered
the ethics of contraception. I believe that we should see this as God's
gift, to be used responsibly; like other gifts from God, it can of course
be used irresponsibly. In other fields like industry and economics, or
medical ethics and technology, Christians have to address questions
which simply did not exist in a previous age.*

*I realise that we have moved on to debate the question of authority.
As an Anglican I want to test fresh ideas first and foremost by
the Bible, acknowledging that there is legitimate debate in many
matters about precisely where it directs us. In the House of Bishops,
the General Synod and the Lambeth Conference, Anglicans go to
work with our tools of Scripture, tradition, reason and experience.
This theological engagement helps us in acknowledging and working
through the complexities we meet in some issues. Our Anglican
view of authority is one which encourages vigorous debate and its
consequences. It permits Christians to live together, even though
they reach, in good conscience, different conclusions. Perhaps we
Anglicans place greater emphasis on freedom of debate, vigorously
tested by Scripture, Tradition, Reason and experience, out of which
firm convictions become received.*

DEREK WORLOCK: I have written before in Better Together *of
authority and its significance as the relationship with the author. The
Catholic Church holds that sacred tradition and sacred Scripture
form one sacred deposit of the word of God, which is committed to the
Church. Vatican II taught that the task of authentically interpreting
the word of God, whether written or handed on, has been entrusted to
the living teaching office of the Church, whose authority is exercised
in the name of Christ. 'Sacred tradition, sacred Scripture and the
teaching authority of the Church, in accord with God's most wise
design, are so linked and joined together that one cannot stand
without the others; and all together and each in its own way under
the action of the one Holy Spirit contribute effectively to the salvation
of souls'* (Divine Revelation, *Article 10).*

We have dealt with this issue at some length in this form of dialogue
to show that we do not shrink from facing our differences, as with
full hearts we pursue the unity of truth. In quoting so much from
documentation and declarations, we emphasise that important issues
cannot be a matter of personal opinion, although clearly, properly
informed personal conscience is a major consideration. Ecumenism
is between Churches rather than simply between individuals, though

individuals have the responsibility of creating the atmosphere of friendship, sharing and enlightenment in which honest assessment and progress become possible. In this sense, such genuine ecumenical enquiry is part of the wider task of evangelisation.

We have been encouraged by the recently published ARCIC (Anglican Roman Catholic International Commission) Report on Morals, Communion and the Church (ARCIC II, 1994). It looks carefully at the official but conflicting pronouncements of our Churches in the areas of marriage, divorce, procreation and contraception. The Report argues that our differences are serious but not fundamental:

> On the subject of contraception we agree that procreation is one of the divinely intended 'goods' of marriage. A deliberate decision therefore without justifiable reason to exclude procreation from a marriage is a rejection of this 'good' and a contradiction of the nature of marriage itself. On this we also agree. We are likewise at one in opposing what has been called a 'contraceptive mentality', that is, a selfish preference for satisfaction over the more demanding 'good' of having and rearing a family. Both Roman Catholics and Anglicans agree too that God calls married couples to 'responsible parenthood'. Situations exist in which a couple would be morally justified in avoiding bringing children into being. Indeed there are some circumstances in which it would be morally irresponsible to do so. On this our two Communions are also agreed.

This Commission's report speaks of its experience in terms which reflect our own efforts at living communion, side by side in prayer, social action and Church collaboration. The members of ARCIC II write:

> Working together has convinced us that the disagreements on moral matters, which at present exist between us, need not constitute an insuperable barrier to progress towards fuller communion. Painful and perplexing as they are, they do not reveal a fundamental divergence in our understanding of the moral implications of the Gospel.

And it sums up:

> Working together on moral issues would be a practical way of expressing the communion we already enjoy, of moving towards full communion and of understanding more clearly what it entails. Without such collaboration we run the risk of increasing

divergence. Moving towards shared witness would contribute significantly to the mission of the Church, and allow the light of the Gospel to shine more fully upon the moral perplexities in today's world.

Government-inspired concern about the teaching of right and wrong has brought public interest once more to bear particularly on Urban Priority Areas. There has been widespread anxiety about young people running wild; about the high proportion growing up in homes with only one parent; about so many boys lacking a male role model. Our Tale of Two Cities made it clear that there are large areas in Merseyside's perimeter estates and in the inner city, where those who achieve well in school, Church, youth club or employment have for generations moved away from the district. We have warned over many years of the danger of creating a community of the 'left-behind' with the accompanying sense of failure that goes with it. That is not to give further currency to the concept of an 'underclass'.

We object to the use of the word 'underclass'; first, because we should only designate groups of people with any sort of label if that is how they characterise themselves. We have described many people as 'working class', knowing that they gladly define themselves that way. We learned to speak of black people because they made it clear they were proud to call themselves black. No persons we know would ever want to describe themselves as members of an underclass, and it could only be damaging to them if they were so described. We object because the idea of an underclass is frequently carried further to support the theory that some people by their own intrinsic nature belong among the non-achievers. The word 'underclass' lends specious authority to old ways of stigmatising, which said things like, 'If you give these people a bath, they'll only put coal in it.' Evangelisation insists that there is good news for demoralised areas: people who have made a bad start in life can be redeemed. It is well worth putting good opportunities in their path; and it is a sin not to try.

Some of our clergy and lay people, with long experience in Urban Priority Areas in Merseyside, make clear to us the scale of the need we face: one clergyman said he is confronted by hard faces of young people in a way he did not meet some twenty years ago. A youth worker said young people he meets have a lot of bravado and not much confidence: 'Washing their face in the morning is a major achievement; their self-esteem is so low.' A Community Liaison Police Officer said most of the young people she meets are so lacking in self-confidence that they would have to surmount a series of major hurdles before they could feel able to go on a Training Scheme. On another estate young people told two clergy who spent time with them, one Anglican, one Roman Catholic,

'Nobody listens to us, so we won't bother talking.' 'Demoralisation' is another word used by a priest to sum up young people's feelings: 'A lack of any sense of possibilities for your own life.'

The connection between demoralisation and moral behaviour may seem complex but it is worth exploring. 'If you feel a nobody, you become a somebody if you are known to be a bomber': that is what we were told about a young man in Belfast. He had left school without any kind of qualification: blew himself up while planting a bomb for the IRA. In demoralised English situations there is no cause such as the IRA claims to put before young people. English young people who feel they are nobodies, become somebodies in the eyes of their peer group by being boldest in defiance, most daredevil with a stolen car, or with drugs or thieving.

It is difficult for many boys to see a wholesome male role model whom they can admire, if we allow areas to become 'communities of the left behind'. We do not want to suggest that there is any one answer to problems which are generations deep. But the connections with mass youth unemployment are inescapable: if you are working with young people in such situations and you want to turn around destructive attitudes, what are the tools you want to have at your disposal? High on the list must be the ability to point to role models who find fulfilment in working hard and who are proud to support a family. Without such examples to appeal to, it is hard to persuade school leavers that it is worth putting their backs into learning skills.

The calling to be a responsible husband and father has a central place in the ethic we proclaim. Changing patterns of employment certainly make that harder to achieve. What used to be the normal challenge to men to be the reliable breadwinners has in many places given way to a context in which the employment which is available offers part-time jobs for women. Down the generations men have not been trained to play other parts.

'Second Chance Learning' in Colleges of Further Education can be the route to new self-confidence, both about personal skills which have been trampled on earlier and about parenting. A Liverpool survey in the 1980s reported parents saying things like, 'I've always wanted my child to do well in school, but didn't know how to support her school learning.' One young woman described her year's course in what is now Liverpool Community College: 'Before I started the course, I was a bored, unemployed and disillusioned single parent, with no job prospects and no ideas on how to pull myself and my son out of the rut that had developed around me. It was my mother who introduced me to the course, herself a student the previous year.'

A young man, who left school with no qualifications at all, believed he would never get over the problems that he had with English. Through adult basic education he now finds them not as difficult to overcome as he had expected. He went on to study on an Access Course, hoping eventually to gain professional employment. And, quite as significantly, he realised he could now be a role model for his children, showing the doors that learning can open and that an 'ordinary person' in the area can 'make it'.

DAVID SHEPPARD: When I completed ten years in Liverpool, people in the Diocese were kind enough to establish an Anniversary Trust for whatever cause I would like. I said I wanted the Trust to make grants in the field of Second Chance Learning. Every quarter we receive between thirty and sixty applications, mostly from people who are desperately poor. I'm told that a grant of £50 or £100 makes all the difference with fares or equipment. Mostly they left school as low achievers. Now the penny has dropped, bringing enthusiasm for learning and the confidence that increasingly goes with it. They are absolutely determined to make the most of themselves and, whenever it is possible, find employment.

The public debate about the teaching of right and wrong came to a head over the tragic and profoundly disturbing murder of the toddler James Bulger by two ten-year-old boys. The day following the verdict, a Government minister, David Maclean, accused the Church of not teaching right and wrong. No doubt he thought he was taking a swipe at 'trendy' bishops and clergy. We were angry at this gibe; we thought about the army of devoted lay people who week in and week out in Church schools, Sunday schools and youth groups are trying to teach right and wrong in ways which youngsters will take on board for themselves. In fact the trial judge saw matters very differently. He said that the two boys concerned did know the meaning of right and wrong, because they had attended a Church of England primary school.

The Church is sometimes accused of being soft on criminals – perhaps that is because evangelisation insists that the Gospel is about forgiveness and new starts. People confuse forgiving with condoning. True forgiveness is very costly, as we see in the Lord's suffering on the Cross. True forgiveness maintains an unswerving hostility to evil. We need to name evils to young people and to ourselves; and there are inhibitions that need strengthening, not weakening, by films and videos we watch – for example, that we would never use violence against a child.

When we were both asked to comment on the James Bulger case, we knew we must include something about the two boys who had killed

James. We made it clear that there were no excuses for the terrible deed done, and that the public must be protected from dangerous young people. But they *can* be redeemed. We insisted that our society must not consign them to the dustbin. There was need for compassion.

Our modern world does not want to admit that primitive and evil forces can be at work in us. But the shocking truth is that evil can enter into people, youngsters or adults. That is why Evangelisation is not just about advice and laws. We know we need the grace of God at work within us.

6

Ground for Hope

Afflictions give ground for endurance, and endurance gives proof of our faith, and a proven faith gives ground for hope (Romans 5:3,4, R. A. Knox translation).

We were together for a public gathering organised by the Wavertree Council of Churches. It had taken the form of a three-man ecumenical Brains Trust. We had had a fair grilling from the lively audience, and had reached that blessed moment when the question-master appeared to have reached the last of the bits of paper passed up from the body of the hall. He read it out slowly and with deliberation: 'What particular benefit has each of you gained from your practice of ecumenism?' 'Good question,' commented our chairman, and turned towards us: 'Now, which of you is going first?' We sidestepped the customary allusion to an opening batsman, and both looked purposefully towards John Newton. We have asked him to try to repeat the answer he gave that evening, and then we will follow.

JOHN NEWTON: Ecumenism is sometimes presented as a kind of ecclesiastical game of beggar-your-neighbour: 'If you give us this, I'll give you that' – for the sake of 'unity'. I believe that whole approach to be spurious and unworthy of those who believe in a God who has set before us the 'unsearchable riches of Christ'. We are not to try to strip one another of our most distinctive treasures, but to share them.

That is not always easy, because in our separation we have grown away from each other, in our confessions of faith and in our patterns of devotion. Ecumenism has taught me, however, that if a belief or practice is precious to my sisters or brothers of another communion, then it behoves me to listen carefully to their testimony.

For me, an important example of this principle is the place of

Mary, the Mother of the Lord, in the whole scheme of salvation. In the Protestant faith in which I was raised, Mary played a relatively minor role. Any attempt to enhance that role was viewed with suspicion, as being likely to detract from the central place of Jesus as Lord and Saviour.

Yet as I learned to listen to Christians of other traditions – High Anglican, Orthodox, Roman Catholic – on their attitude to Mary, my own understanding changed. I have come to see that, in a religion of the Word made flesh, Mary's role, as the Mother of the Lord, is crucial. She opens herself to the life-giving Spirit of God, and co-operates with his gracious purpose, in the complete simplicity of her response of faith and love: 'Be it unto me according to thy word.'

The child born to her is born of the Spirit of God, but he is also bone of her bone and flesh of her flesh. Nor is that a merely biological bond between them. Dr Frank Lake and Clinical Theology caused me to reflect on the profound significance of the mother–child relationship. Mothers are the makers of spirit, as the saying goes. The love and care of the mother is formative for the whole personal, moral and spiritual development of the child.

I must then take seriously that fact that Jesus is not just 'born of a woman' in an abstract sense, but is 'Mary's son'. He grows up a whole person, his humanity is integral and unspoilt by sin and selfishness. That being so, and if mothers are indeed the makers of spirit, then the utter goodness of Jesus says something quite overwhelming about Mary's mothering of him.

I am encouraged, as a Protestant Christian, by the Second Vatican Council's forthright declaration that the honour due to Mary as the handmaid of the Lord can, 'Neither take away from nor add anything to the dignity and efficacy of Christ the one Mediator.' Thanks to ecumenism, however, I have learned to reverence and love her.

DEREK WORLOCK: From experience on other similar occasions, I knew my stock answer almost by heart. The main benefit lay in the newly improved relations with other Christians since our mutual recognition of the validity of each other's baptism. This had enabled us to share the work of the Gospel which Christ had left to his followers. But that was something we had all shared; and the questioner was asking for a more personal or particular benefit that I had gained. So I decided to surprise the audience by admitting that for me probably the biggest 'plus' was my discovery of the richness and relevance of God's word in Holy Scripture. To some extent this had been occasioned by the emphasis placed on the word in the teachings of the Second Vatican Council. Ecumenically, this had often been at the heart of what I was now able to share with those who did not necessarily share the fullness of my faith.

True enough, in days when I was studying in the seminary, time and due prominence had been given to the Scriptures; but the focus was firmly on the New Testament, especially the Gospels. For the Old Testament the treatment was primarily academic, and the Bible as such was often referred to as 'The Closed Book' where Catholics were concerned. Things were just stirring at the time of my ordination to the priesthood, and the war-time work of Mgr Ronald Knox in his translation of the New Testament was historic, though still treated with suspicion. The Douay Version had been in sole possession for so long, more than three hundred years, that the language and style had come to seem almost essential, even though dated and open to misunderstanding of its imagery.

Now we listened to the Knox version as to a new book. This was especially true of the Pauline letters. But the very freshness of the version led to some suspicions, which became an even greater obstacle when the translation of the Old Testament had been completed. The Knox New Testament was published with the authority of all our bishops in England and Wales in 1945, but four years later only Cardinal Griffin at Westminster was prepared to authorise the translation of the Old Testament. It was not until 1955 that the Knox Bible in its entirety was fully authorised and published. Much of the difficulty was the lack of familiarity with the Law and the Prophets. I well remember hearing Cardinal Heenan say, 'The God of the Old Testament was tribal God'. But the real throwback was the inherited belief that the New Testament was for Catholics and the Old Testament for Protestants.

In a sense it was the introduction of the vernacular into our liturgy, with the availability first of the Knox Version and then of the even more spectacular Jerusalem Bible, which opened up for Roman Catholics in this country an appreciation of the Word. This was particularly significant when seen in relation to our revised liturgy of the Eucharist, when after the readings from Scripture the celebrant is encouraged each day to give a short homily in exposition of the passages which have been read. I have found it to be a most valuable learning experience, strengthening devotion as well as understanding. I dare to say that at the Reformation, the Reformers lost the Eucharist, and the adherents to the Catholic religion in general lost the Word. The marvel of ecumenism is that both are at last in the process of recovery. Therein lies real hope for our coming together: our communion in Christ. It has already been a long pilgrimage, but our rediscovery of the Word, Old Testament and New, has been encouragement and reinvigoration. It has been greatly helped by our recognising how much the Bible has meant to our fellow-pilgrims. For me personally it has been an overwhelming benefit.

DAVID SHEPPARD: My answer at Wavertree was that I had learned, especially from Roman Catholics, how suffering can itself be a way of serving God. In the past I had jibbed at any suggestion that we can share in Christ's sufferings. The Protestant in me was jealous to protect the truth of the once-for-all suffering of Christ for the sins of the world. Indeed, I remember at one stage saying that the symbol of Christianity was not a Crucifix, but an empty Cross.

Today I believe as passionately as I ever did that Jesus, the innocent Lamb of God, suffered alone on the cross as a sacrifice for the sins of all humankind: none of us can share in that sacrifice. No one would have argued that more clearly than St Paul, yet he wrote, 'I am now rejoicing in my sufferings for your sake, and in my flesh I am completing what is lacking in Christ's afflictions for the sake of his body, that is, the church' (Colossians 1:24). I have seen partners, parents, colleagues, friends, take the strain and suffer for others as part of God's way of deliverance.

I have come to share gladly with Derek in presenting two joint churches with a Crucifix for their east wall. It properly stands for the Lord's continuing suffering alongside us in a world full of grief and pain, as well as for that unique, once-for-all sacrifice for our sins. And I have learned from Roman Catholics that there is a vocation to suffering: that makes it possible for those who bear constant pain to see something creative in their lives.

There is a danger that an attitude of resignation and submission can lead to sitting down under suffering: sometimes Jesus' response to pain, illness and injustice was blazing indignation. Often today, a refusal to give in can play a major part in healing. The Crucifix witnesses to a willingness to receive from the Father whatever he allows, and to respond to his calling, so that attitudes and the course of events itself can be changed.

What right have those of us who are healthy and comfortable to tell those whose life seems one long tale of suffering that there is good news? We need a portion of that indignation which Jesus showed at the presence of sickness, handicap or injustice in God's good world. Our response must include doing whatever is in our power to stand with people, and to bring about change in their circumstances. If then the suffering continues, we do have a right to tell them of the transforming love of Christ. And, marvellously, we see then how he can take the raw material of suffering and transform it into great beauty of character.

These three testimonies speak of ways in which the openness of our relationship with other Christians has been an enrichment for each of us. We have stopped feeling threatened by the others: we expect to learn from their distinctive understandings as we journey together in life's pilgrimage. This points to a unity in which a certain diversity is possible and may flourish, where we do not ask others to set aside particular insights, but to hold them in trust, perhaps for the subsequent enrichment of all of us. It is a fact that 'openness' can do much to improve relationships. In his visit to Liverpool in 1982 Pope John Paul remarked that 'ecumenism is not just of the intellect; it is also of the affections'. Openness in ecumenical matters not only promotes greater intellectual understanding; it is a necessary preliminary to improved human relations, and gives extra meaning to Christian fellowship.

We have often written or spoken before now of the importance of 'being there'. In a simple and humble way we have to try to reflect the wonder of the Incarnation, through which the Son of God came to share our human life in order to show us how to live and work, and to enable us to be drawn into playing our part in his unique act of redeeming the world. We have to try to be a sign of charity, hope and justice, where it matters. At the same time Christ is not exclusively our possession. We must also seek to recognise him in the world, amid the circumstances, good or bad, in which people today have to work out their salvation.

This 'being there' can be both a personal thing, and it can also involve the recognition of the Gospel as having relevance to real life today. A bishop has to try to 'be there' to his clergy in their life and ministry, just as they must try to 'be there' to the people they are called to serve. For the bishop, it cannot be merely a form of personal commitment involving occasional physical presence. This may at times be neither practical nor even desirable, though he needs to make sure that his circumstances are not too remote from those who represent him in their ministry. The bishop's 'being there' to his priests is often very necessary for the sympathetic affirmation required by those taking the strain at the coal-face. Though he cannot always be with them, they need to be confident that he really appreciates their situation. His understanding and support, however given, will help bring strength, perseverance, encouragement, and even an ability to endure in face of hurtful difficulties, stress, domestic worries and 'burn-out'. This is especially true in cases where those charged with pastoral ministry feel threatened by hardships and events beyond their control or choosing.

For us this personal commitment to those 'in the field' is a major consideration. As bishops, we have particular responsibilities where our clergy are concerned. This is especially true when perhaps priests may feel that they are struggling against the odds to achieve some pastoral strategy, apparently carried through all too easily elsewhere. Unchecked, this can lead to the weariness, frustration and desperation which are the outward signs of physical or spiritual 'burn-out'. Ecumenical neighbours can sometimes be a most welcome support, but needs differ.

In the Anglican Diocese a scheme of Appraisal in Ministry is now firmly established: the Bishop conducts their Appraisal with senior staff and Area Deans, the Area Deans with parochial clergy. In that case an agreed summary of the conversation comes to the Bishop: he sweats over writing a thoughtful letter to each person following the Appraisal. Quite often this process brings to the surface matters that clergy and bishop need to talk about face to face. On the other hand the Roman Catholic Archdiocese at one time tried to arrange for a scheme where one priest would watch over another finding the 'going' tough. The scheme was soon nicknamed 'mutual minders', and something much less organised exists more effectively today. But a counselling service for clergy under stress is increasingly necessary.

Clergy suffering stress are not the only pillars of faith under strain in today's very secular world of public life and business. The priest can sometimes find himself under great pressure for having had the courage to recommend a stand against the common trend or popular opinion. This hostility can range from the taunting 'Evening, Vicar' from the group on the street corner, to the brick through his window or misrepresentation by the media. When in his anxiety he remembers that the flag he carries is that of the Lord, he is even more conscious of his need to 'get it right'. But only his circumstances are different from those of lay people such as a shop-steward, whose members are threatened with redundancy. He too is concerned with justice, and may be in great need of moral support from the clergy, as he foresees the likely demands of management following the introduction of advanced technology or new working practices. To 'be there' at such a moment of impending crisis may well be an even more important part of Christian mission in the future.

As the demands of advancing technology and the globalisation of market forces become steadily more complex, there will be an increasing excuse for a bishop or priest to plead that giving advice and judgment in such matters is beyond his competence. He finds himself in danger of saying: '*You* carry the faith into your world, and *we* will pray for you in ours.' It may not be expressed as crudely as that, but undoubtedly in many parts of the country today, the separation of the two worlds can lead to just such alienation or apathetic indifference. Yet the integrity of the Christian Gospel always has light to cast on human problems, questions of business ethics and social justice. The humanity of Christ enables us to reach out to sustain the victims of tragedy and disaster, and to offer the support of 'presence', listening and understanding to those whose sometimes unconscious faith can come under challenge. In this respect the almost unique character of Liverpool and its people has taught us much.

We had not been here for long before we began to appreciate the quite remarkable degree to which religion is integrated into the life of the city. It was never more obvious than at the time of the two football disasters of the 1980s, at the Heysel Stadium in Brussels in 1985, and at the Hillsborough ground in Sheffield in 1989. The Heysel tragedy produced a widespread sense of guilt in the city, since it was as a result of pre-match hooliganism, in which Liverpool supporters were prominent, that a wall collapsed and a number of spectators, mostly Italian, were crushed to death. Though by no means all those involved were from Liverpool, there was great distress in the city. Services were held in both our Cathedrals, at which the team, its supporters, government ministers, ambassadors and civic leaders took part. Our task was to lead the city in both mourning and penitence. Some days later we accompanied a group of city fathers and football team officers to Turin to express Liverpool's condolences to the bereaved. With the Cardinal Archbishop of Turin, we took part in a service in that city's principal shrine, La Consolata, where we both preached with the help of an expert Vatican interpreter. Even the Militant Labour leaders of the City Council, who had requested our company in the delegation, seemed glad to have the Church with them that evening.

The feeling in Liverpool, following the Hillsborough disaster in 1989, was quite different: a city in mourning, with genuine shared sorrow for ninety-six Liverpool supporters, crushed to death in one of the stands where they had gone for the FA Cup Semi-final. The whole ghastly spectacle had been shown on television as it happened. In answer to a call for assistance, we sent a team of chaplains to help the bereaved and the injured in the Sheffield hospitals. On the Sunday evening we were together in Liverpool's Catholic Cathedral for a Mass, attended by a crowd of many thousands. A further overflow Mass was celebrated outside. It was suggested to those standing there that they might go home and watch it on television. But no, they stayed, standing together to witness to their solidarity with their mates who had died the previous afternoon. Many of the supporters brought their red and white football scarves with them, and soon the first of the flower-strewn shrines began to be created. That night in the Cathedral a blue-clad Evertonian sang 'You'll never walk alone' alongside a red-scarfed Liverpool supporter. When a radio reporter commented on this, he received the reply 'We're all Liverpool tonight.'

For a full fortnight the city went into mourning. During the first week a seemingly unending line of supporters wound its way around the Anfield Football Ground, to leave flowers, scarves, favours and even crib figures on the pitch. After a few days half the ground was covered, every railing in the Kop festooned with Liverpool colours. The Football Club asked us, together with John Newton, to come to the ground on three occasions that week to help with prayers, but mostly with presence and support. Meantime, the city, like a great family in bereavement, was preparing for the individual funerals. These took place the following week and were attended by large crowds. Liverpool Football Club itself gave a splendid example by sending one of its players or its manager, Kenny Dalglish, to each funeral, and it also showed great initiative in helping with the provision of counselling services. It was soon evident that these were needed not just for the families directly bereaved, but for some of the many thousands who were present at Hillsborough or who were traumatised by what they had witnessed on television as the tragedy unfolded before their eyes.

DEREK WORLOCK: One young man returned home from Hillsborough in tears and completely dazed. He sat and sat and did not want to do anything. His wife put on the television set for the Requiem Mass from the Metropolitan Cathedral. At last something stirred him and the Counselling Services sent him to see me some days later. He told me that some words I had used in my sermon had brought him out of that deep pit. I wondered what theological insight had proved so important. It turned out to be something much more ordinary, but realistic. I had described visiting injured fans in hospital in Sheffield and said that the Yorkshire nurses were becoming used to their patients saying, 'Thanks, luv, for the bevvy.' It was yet another example of the Lord's love reaching people within their own particular culture.

The mourning period came to an end with another great service, this time in the Anglican Cathedral. Many will remember its simple conclusion, with a choirboy singing the song which had been on everyone's lips in the preceding days: 'You'll never walk alone'. The various lines of what had for some years been the anthem of the Liverpool football supporters achieved an enriched and undying significance at that time. It has given us the title for this book.

DAVID SHEPPARD: A year later we were asked back again to the Anfield ground for a service to mark the first anniversary of the disaster, which marvellously turned out to be Easter Day. At that service I made the point that it was all right for fans from the football terraces to weep and to find help in counselling. The specially opened Hillsborough Counselling Centre was put under such pressure after that service, which was seen on television, that for the first time in twelve months the counsellors could only see people if they had made an appointment. In other more personal ways, Liverpool did much for its own healing after Hillsborough: people admitted their grief and openly showed their support and care. One friend found herself given a big hug when she went into work. Her colleague said to her, 'I've decided to show people now how much I care for them, not wait till after they are dead, and then tell everyone how much I valued them.'

100

The initiative in 'being there', as expressed in Liverpool's two football tragedies, required both availability and restraint. It was important on both occasions that the Church should not seem to 'take over' the mourning, grief and mutual support which were expressed so naturally and wholeheartedly by the people. It was yet another example of what, in *Better Together*, we referred to as the almost unconscious faith of many who may well not be church-goers:

> Whether we call this phenomenon our unconscious faith or a feeling after God, a rumour of God or an echo of his voice, there seems little doubt that some toe-hold of faith and Christian values remains. In many deprived areas, shared hardships and discrimination can produce a remarkable degree of solidarity. Being 'members one of another' becomes a living reality in such circumstances . . .

Church leaders are also part of that one body, and being there in times of joy and tragedy is an important part of recognising Christ's presence, incarnate in the reality of people's lives. But our heavenly Father did not protect Jesus from suffering and human weakness: nor has he promised to protect us. When such trials and tribulations have touched us personally, it has not been easy for us to recognise God's saving power in our human sufferings.

DEREK WORLOCK: When in July 1992 I was unexpectedly diagnosed as having lung cancer, the surgeon told me that now I had a new means of speaking up for a large number of silent men and women in Merseyside where there is exceptionally high incidence of this disease. So the nature of my complaint was immediately made public, with details of the surgery carried out and the months of chemotherapy which followed. I was told plainly the very low percentage of those who survived three months. Strangely I did not feel unduly fearful of death itself, though I was distressed at the thought of those I must leave behind and of what seemed at the time important work left unfinished.

The pain was not inconsiderable, though the nausea from the chemotherapy was worse. I was wonderfully well supported personally and by my doctors during the long struggle to recover energy and strength, but the greatest trial was the inability to concentrate. This deprived me of any satisfaction from prayer. David was among those who encouraged me to leave the praying to others. Almost everyone who came to see me recited the Lord's Prayer. I remained cold as a stone spiritually and desperately troubled by nightmares. With one entire lung removed, I had persistent pain in my neck and shoulders. With the rib-cage cut through, my left side felt worse than when I had torn all the inter-costal muscles in my days playing Rugby Football. To keep up my spirits when I came out of hospital, I visited a different parish each day, nestling in a car full of cushions. But at night, the neck, shoulders and side continued to plague me and to keep me awake.

People seemed surprised, even encouraged, by the fact that I found it so difficult to pray. One night I wrote a Pastoral Letter for reading in all the parishes. It was about my bedroom at Archbishop's House, and about two pictures on my bedroom wall:

'One is the first picture of Our Lady I ever saw: my mother's rather majestic picture of the Blessed Virgin Mary, on a throne, carrying her child. The other is a very realistic picture of Christ hanging on the cross. It is the line-sketch upon which the Spanish artist, Salvador Dali, based his famous painting of "Christ of St John of the Cross". This hangs over the head of my bed, and on the opposite wall is a large mirror. So, from my bed, I see reflected the crucified Christ, arms nailed and stretched out above me. I have had this picture there for many years, and my prayer has been that one day the outstretched arms will enfold me in their eternal embrace.

'Many of you will know the painting I mean. Sketched from above, it gives us a powerful picture of our Lord's suffering, especially through the agonised twisted muscles of his neck and shoulders, bearing his asphyxiated body. It shows us the extent to which Jesus shared our humanity, what the Incarnation ultimately meant for Him, and what can be involved for us if we are to be "conformed to Christ", and try to share in the work of redeeming the world.

'I am sure you can guess with what feeling in the last few weeks I have looked at the reflection of those torn muscles and the spear-hole in the side of Christ. It has helped me to understand what he accepted as part of the human suffering asked of him as our Redeemer, and just a little of what may be offered to us as one way of our sharing in the task of redeeming the world. Sometimes the difficulty can be that, even when our faith and belief remain firm, the pursuit of warm personal devotion can seem fruitless and can leave our human heart without the consolation we seek. It is as if our Lord is sharing with us his cry from the cross: "My God, my God, why have you forsaken me?"

'That is the challenge of our faith. Of course, the easy answer is for us to dismiss such thoughts of our imitation of Christ by saying simply "It was different for him". Indeed it was, for he is the Son of God. But he chose to share our griefs and sorrows. Our own sufferings and difficulties can seem cruel and pointless unless they are related to the work of salvation. In our hearts we know that properly directed, they can be a way in which we are drawn into the life and purpose of our Saviour. That is never easy for us but it is part of our faith.

It is expressed each day by the priest at Mass when he prays: "May we come to share in the divinity of Christ, who humbled himself to share in our humanity."'

Although we managed, with Grace Sheppard and John Newton, to see each other often, and John Furnival was constantly at hand to help with communication and to pick up outstanding points, nevertheless for some months we both had to relearn particular forms of ministry and witness, which we had shared on an almost daily basis for more than fifteen years. David had to undertake speaking engagements where the original booking was for both of us. Derek, as he has explained, had a new and lone form of ministry to experience. It was six months before we managed to appear together and preach again with John Newton. Suitably enough that was for the annual service for the Week of Prayer for Christian Unity, held in January that year at Wigan. It was from about that time that the planning of this book began to take shape. We both realised how much we valued the resources that come from facing matters together, whether they be grave or glad.

DAVID SHEPPARD: There is a certain isolation inherent in the task of being a bishop. We both have colleagues in our own Church, whose support is worth a king's ransom. Yet we have both found there were times when the person bearing parallel responsibilities in the same place understands more deeply what the pressures are. These include the particular pain which a bishop knows of personal tragedies or moral lapses of clergy, and of near despair when high hopes have been dashed for a wider community in which we have both been involved. We have shared these with each other. Because of our public involvement together and of many unhurried private conversations, we think we have grown to be a little wiser and a little braver. We have learned the value of an affirming telephone call when a selective report in the media has been tantamount to misrepresentation, opening the way to criticism. We have learned that in the responsibilities we share, we too need to 'be there' for one another.

Derek has written about his illness, which included some very dark nights, when those of us closest to him could only be there, our presence perhaps a reminder of the love and risen power of Christ. I have not had to face that sort of dark night so far on my personal journey. But being there with someone close in their suffering brings its own kind of pain for the one who watches. In 1957, soon after we were married, Grace experienced a nervous breakdown, leading eventually to long years of agoraphobia. I felt very bewildered, not understanding what was happening or how to help. I could only stay with her, assuring her that she was loved and wanted. Looking back, with Grace having for years lived a full and demanding life, I regard that time as a major growth point in my understanding of how vulnerable we human beings are.

Later, in 1965, I was told that she had no more than a 50–50 chance of living for as long as five years: this was as she left hospital after major surgery for cancer and weeks of radiotherapy. Some days I felt resigned to loss, not knowing what God was doing with us. And there were visits to the hospital, when I was clearly the weaker partner, needing to be strengthened by the patient. These times have helped me to learn patience, to respect the dignity of the sufferer and not to demand answers to all the questions. Derek's recent illness brought many of those feelings back, with the need to stay close in human companionship, believing him to be in God's loving hands even during those dark nights.

In these Liverpool years there have been other times when hope seems to have been reduced to no more than a tiny flicker. Part of the privilege for me of 'being there' has been that at times people who have felt themselves powerless, disregarded by those in power, have opened their hearts. One evening in Kirkby a member of such a group looked straight at me and said, 'You know these powerful people. Why don't you tell them how it is?' It was as though the whole weight of generations of disadvantage was being loaded on to my head.

Sometimes doors to government ministers or business magnates have opened. Media interviews or House of Lords debates have given opportunities to speak publicly. I have tried to tell what I have seen and heard, only to find such attempts at witness being dismissed simply as my political stance or as naïve lack of knowledge of the way the world has to be. Derek's presence with me on some of those occasions has been a great support, sometimes helping me to laugh at myself: 'You had your shining armour on today'; sometimes helping me to face failure without losing hope. Once we found ourselves in the street after seeing a government minister: we had stood our ground after a rather humiliating attempt to put us in our place and the rejection of the case we were trying to make for some particular needs of Merseyside. When we reached the street, Derek took a deep breath of London air, shook himself, and said, 'I feel clean.'

We had not sought that confrontation: we have always tried to remember that, though speaking our minds may relieve our own feelings, we are there to win a hearing which may change the circumstances of life for people who have no voice. These have been dark years for many in Merseyside: I feel indignant that they have so little share in the opportunities of what is, in world terms, a very prosperous country. 'Comfortable Britain' does not want to share those opportunities, if there is any risk of losing some of its own advantages. So it is hard to be optimistic. We have learned to encourage each other with the truth that hope reaches beyond success or failure.

We discovered quite early on that when it comes to collaboration between the Churches, it does not make for trusting relationships if one Church makes firm plans, and then invites the others to join in an 'ecumenical' service or project. It became a principle for us that we need to start from the base-line together: there we ask if each wants to be part of shared plans, and on what basis. Sometimes one Church, having the appropriate resources in staff, contacts or money, will act as 'Lead Church'. At times, two Churches can plan a project together; at other times, all the Covenanting Churches must share, if possible from the beginning. There are also times when other Churches, who do not feel able to join in a Covenant, will be willing to share in particular projects. Whichever structure is chosen, keeping others in the picture by good communications helps to keep trust strong. It is important, for example, that Church Leaders should not be taken by surprise when significant national or diocesan projects organised by other Churches are made public. We need to keep each other posted about pieces of work being done in our Church and about possible plans that are under consideration. Good communications are also the key when we discover that bad feelings are around.

If going back to the base-line to make plans together is one principle, another is to make no private deals. In 1992 an example of the old mistrust started to emerge from the woodwork: negotiations to appoint a full-time Anglican chaplain to a new National Health Trust Hospital led to resentment and to a public protest by one priest about disproportionately less resources being given to Roman Catholic chaplains serving there. For a time there was even unofficial talk of a 'work to rule'. Less publicly there were some sharp remarks about the chaplains from one Church being regularly called out at night (with the assumption that the others were not); and counterclaims that some stayed for a long time counselling bereaved families (with the implication that the others simply provided hurried words and actions). There was also a fear that the appointment of a full-time Established Church chaplain might affect the status of other clergy working on a part-time basis.

David therefore wrote a letter to Derek, setting out the history, as he saw it, of hospital chaplaincies in Merseyside, and of previous discussions in which we had been involved about ways of collaboration. We then discussed the issue openly on two occasions with the Roman Catholic Vicar General and the Anglican Archdeacon, who were responsible in each Church for hospital chaplaincies. Those consultations helped to underline the different approaches which clergy from the two Churches often brought to hospital chaplaincy. At the first meeting David said he was going to meet the Chairman of the Trust

Hospital, but he promised to enter into no deals until he had reported back and we had reached agreement. After that conversation with the chairman had taken place, David communicated to Derek and the two diocesan officials what had passed between them. Another meeting with the chairman and officers of the Regional Health Authority helped release some new cash for the appointment of chaplains; and eventually a parity of resource was offered. It was further agreed that the Vicar General should join the panel to appoint the Anglican chaplain. Equal standing in the hospital set-up was to be given to the senior priest from among the team of parochial clergy, which was the preferred Roman Catholic way of providing chaplaincy. When difficulties, tensions and apparently discriminatory practices surface, they should be faced, and trouble taken to establish agreed working practices for the future.

This open approach to what may be regarded as administrative difficulties, and sometimes the consequences of ecumenism in social matters, must also be applied to the doctrinal issues which lie at the heart of our differences. It is not helpful to deny or to ignore their existence: they call for openness and trust. We have already said that often these differences prove to be less profound than is generally believed if they are faced up to and examined without animosity. Such an examination requires honesty, trust and confidence that while the approach must be within the context of the Church's teaching, loyalty and integrity are not at stake. Personal relationships may colour the process of dialogue, and even foster the desire to continue searching for a solution to an apparently irresolvable problem. But ecumenism is not a private agreement between individuals. Churches are involved, and an individual cannot ignore or play down some difficult aspect of teaching or discipline just because it does not appeal to him or seems of unlikely consequence to his personal agenda. Honesty as well as honour is at stake here. Mutual trust requires frankness as well as sensitivity. Friendship is not well served by the suppression of truth. It acknowledges the rightness of adherence to a properly informed conscience. It drives the true ecumenist on when progress seems slow, if not actually blocked. Above all it is motivated by the love of Christ who has called his followers to be one.

Although we can look back with great thankfulness for the God-given advances of the past thirty years or more, it would be idle to pretend that there have not been periods of tension between our Churches: times when official exchanges have seemed like a bucket of cold water; high spots like the visit of Pope John Paul to Canterbury and to both our Cathedrals in Liverpool, giving rise to hopes that to many have seemed only partly fulfilled; determined efforts by media prophets of doom to use leaked documents to forecast a mass exodus from one Church to the other. At such times faithful ecumenists have had to keep their heads, avoid hurtful throwaway repartee, and try to recognise what new opportunities for genuine long-term progress are being offered us by our 'God of Surprises', who does not always follow our best-thought-out strategies.

Perhaps the most important and stressful example of such periods of tension has been the months following the decision reached by the Church of England General Synod in November 1992 regarding the ordination of women priests. We had discussed this issue at some length in *Better Together* (chap. 5), so we were aware of our differences on the matter and the grounds on which our views were based. Others shared that knowledge, and we were ourselves conscious of the mounting tension as the issue was discussed in the dioceses and different views were expressed. Some attacked the protagonists for feminism, others spoke in terms of conscience and human rights. Rome re-stated its position that neither the Roman Catholic nor the Orthodox Churches felt competent to alter the unbroken tradition of ordaining only men to the presbyterate and episcopate. A decision by the Church of England to ordain women priests, it was said, would be a severe obstacle to the furtherance of Christian unity.

Clearly, the decision to be reached by the Synod at Church House, Westminster, would be seen as a serious test of our enduring commitment to the road towards unity. The tension was not confined to us. A senior Roman Catholic priest of the Archdiocese told us how he had heard two much younger priests speaking gleefully of the differences which seemed to wrack much of the Anglican community at that time. 'Thank God,' said one to the other, 'this should put an end once and for all to all that talk about ecumenism.' The older man spoke with great feeling later of his own sense of personal enrichment through his close friendship with a number of Anglicans and with Christians of other Churches. 'It was almost as if the younger generation were rejoicing at the pain which the Church of England was experiencing as it tried to hold together.' It was an alarming warning-signal for the future which we hoped was not typical. But it showed how important our own reaction would be to what seemed almost inevitable after the long period of debate.

Half-an-hour after the decisive vote had been announced in the General Synod, David rang Derek in Liverpool, where he was recovering from his cancer operation. We spent a good time talking through how this decision felt for each of us. Later that evening Derek issued the following statement in answer to persistent enquiries from the press:

> The decision reached by the General Synod of the Church of England came as no surprise, and I know well the agonising of many Anglicans about its possible consequences. My reaction is at best mixed. I deeply regret the additional obstacle it constitutes to the fullness of unity I earnestly desire between our Church and

the Church of England. But I know also the conscientious urgings felt by Bishop David and others to an extent which could not be ignored.

Because of the continuing bond of baptism which we enjoy, we must all endeavour to work together to spread and exemplify the good news of the gospel. One has sympathy with those who are anxious to have the matter of women and orders off their agenda so that we may concentrate on the task of evangelising our very secular world. This will have the effect of drawing us closer to mutual understanding and to a solution to this problem of orders, which for the time being defies us.

The final rule for ecumenical dialogue is that when all else fails, all we can do is to offer our endeavours and hurt to God. This we must do by prayer and sharing in the work of the Gospel: by faith, hope and charity: by building on the Christian friendship and partnership which in Merseyside has replaced the sectarian hatreds of old.

In some ways it might have been easier if it had been possible to leave matters there. But as months went by and rumours abounded about the so-called 'Roman Option' facing those opposed to the General Synod's decision, sections of the Press seemed intent upon turning the 'undoubted obstacle' into bitter mutual recrimination. Great care was taken by the leadership of the Churches to ensure that this did not happen; but the uncertainty about the numbers involved, which were by no means consistent throughout the country, helped to fuel rumour and misunderstanding. It was the question whether the Church of England had the authority to make its decision about women and the priesthood which was at the heart of the anxieties which were being expressed, not the issue of feminism or misogyny, as was sometimes alleged.

In their paper *Being in Communion*, the Church of England House of Bishops said:

In a divided Christendom there is no possibility of making decisions in a General Council. Any decisions, therefore, touching the faith or order of the Universal Church need to acknowledge the possibility of error and be offered for testing within the wider ecumenical fellowship . . . The Church of England made its decision to ordain women to the priestly ministry of the Church of God as one part of the Universal Church, using its own decision-making structures, in consultation with the wider Anglican Communion and in knowledge of the different practices of its ecumenical partners. Discernment is now to be seen within the whole Church under the Spirit's guidance (*Being in Communion*, G. S. Misc. 418, 1993, paras 13 and 20).

The Roman Catholic bishops expressed their desire to respond with understanding to the difficulties of those opposed to the Synod's decision. They stated that they were ready to face up to the challenge presented by married Anglican clergy who might be seeking ordination in a Church where the discipline was of celibacy. But the bishops made it plain to those who approached them that, whatever arrangement might be called for in the short term, they would look towards eventual total integration into the Catholic church. This was not a matter which could be rushed, and there was need for discussion within and between both Churches. The Archbishops of Canterbury and York responded swiftly and positively to this suggestion, and a Joint Commission was set up between the Church of England House of Bishops and the Roman Catholic Bishops' Conference.

Even at that time, when the media seemed determined to achieve a head-on clash between our Churches, the Roman Catholic bishops reiterated their continuing commitment to the dialogue, which had been known in recent decades. 'We see,' they wrote in their statement of April 1993, 'that there is a distinction, but no real opposition, between the acceptance of those seeking full communion with the Catholic Church and continuing ecumenical dialogue, since both proceed from the marvellous ways of God.' The Archbishops of Canterbury and York responded that they shared this perception of recent progress, adding, 'We value the imperfect communion which we already share and remain enthusiastically committed to deepening that communion, so that together we may more effectively proclaim the Gospel to our society' (*Lambeth Palace Statement*, 23 April 1993).

Not that it was all plain sailing. As the date for the first ordinations of women priests drew near, the focus tended to shift to named individuals, bishops and well-known laity. If privacy was preserved and information withheld, the charge was of subterfuge and secrecy. If names reached the media, there were often exchanges which did little to help.

On the one hand there would be allegations of triumphalism, and on the other deep hurt would be caused by the use of words like 'defection' and 'sect'. Generalised references to two-way traffic, while in some measure true, served merely as an invitation to ingenious reporters to trail more names. There was at least one notable exception. *The Tablet*, commenting on the reception into the Roman Catholic Church of the Duchess of Kent, said that she was likely to celebrate the forthcoming Week of Prayer for Christian Unity with special fervour: 'Her move from Canterbury to Rome was exemplary. No banging of the door, no beating of the triumphalist big drum, no rejection of the Church she was leaving, only a sense of home-coming in the Catholic Church.' The editorial summed it up: 'The conversion of England remains a task for all the Churches in this country' (*The Tablet*, 15 January 1994).

There can have been few periods in the last century when ecumenical relationships were placed under greater strain. Richard Harries, Bishop of Oxford, judged that 'the relationship that has been built up over 25 years between the Roman Catholic Church and the Church of England has been put to the test and found strong. The present disagreement over the ordination of women to the priesthood by the Anglican Church, far from destroying the relationship, has in fact revealed its desirability' (*The Tablet*, 12 March 1994). Yet for all the welcome lack of animosity, we would not wish to play down the stress and genuine heartache felt by many: their sense of loss or estrangement, matched to a degree by the challenge experienced by others, who found themselves needing to adapt some of their attitudes and traditions to accommodate the spirituality and customs of those seeking to join them.

Amid much generosity and heart-searching, some hurts were undoubtedly sustained by members of both Churches. Some highly sensitive issues have still to be resolved. Even when certain personality problems and difficulties of individuals have been eased, there remains the 'severe obstacle' to unity, which Roman Catholics fear was caused by the decision of the Church of England Synod in 1992 and the subsequent ordinations of women. These first ordinations were held in the spring of 1994 amid enthusiasm and rejoicing in the Church of England. At the same time, for the guidance of Roman Catholics, Pope John Paul reaffirmed that 'the Church has no authority whatsoever to confer priestly ordination on women' (Apostolic Exhortation *Ordinatio Sacerdotalis*, 22 May 1994). The 'severe obstacle', as it had been called earlier, clearly remains weighty and real, and there were some who questioned the purpose of continuing dialogue.

Yet remarkably, amid all this acknowledged difference and difficulty, we detect some positive growth and development with regard to the all-important issue of communion. The Second Vatican Council had spoken of the real but imperfect communion existing between all those properly baptised. The depth of that bond between our two Churches was spelt out in the Common Declaration, issued by Pope John Paul II and Archbishop Robert Runcie on 2 October 1989: 'This communion already shared is grounded in faith in God our Father, in our Lord Jesus Christ, and in the Holy Spirit; our common baptism into Christ; our sharing of the Holy Scriptures, of the Apostles' and Nicene Creeds; the Chalcedonian definition and teaching of the Fathers; our common inheritance for many centuries.' Yet the century-old judgment of Leo XIII on Anglican Orders remains a source of great sadness to us; and until it has proved possible for this to be reconsidered and perhaps left in the past, there seems no way forward regarding the eucharistic hospitality desired by many.

It is against this remaining and still painful background that we find comfort and hope in the charity and friendship in the exchanges and joint consultations which have marked what would otherwise have had to be regarded as a severe setback to ecumenical relations. There was a real danger of reversion to the earlier position of 'absolutely right versus absolutely wrong'. Instead new insights and new emphases have appeared which we sincerely hope may lighten the way ahead, especially on this important issue of Orders. We do not wish this contemporary crisis over women and the priesthood to dominate the whole question of our approach to Christian Unity, which must include not only the question of primacy, but the meaning of legitimate diversity among members of the one body of Christ, the Church. Some people in the ecumenical movement seem to be giving up the search for visible unity in favour of occasional co-operation and a loose form of commitment. We both continue to hope and pray that our Churches, at present engaged alongside each other in the life of the Gospel, may be moving forward along convergent, not parallel lines. We cannot foresee precisely the shape of things to come, but we pray that we may be truly one Church. It is this which we mean when we speak of meeting in Christ, and it was this which we believe was the mind of those who signed the Swanwick Declaration in 1987.

DEREK WORLOCK: As just one example of the 'new emphases and insights', let me quote from the statement issued by the Roman Catholic Bishops' Conference of England and Wales in April 1994, after due consultation with the Holy See:

It has become clear that a key question for many who are approaching us is the view they should take of the sacramental life they have faithfully lived as members of the Church of England. This is an important question for our Catholic community, too. It is the clear teaching of the Second Vatican Council that visible elements of the Church of Christ can and do exist outside the boundaries of the Catholic Church. The visible elements and sacred actions spoken of by the Conciliar Decree on Ecumenism, include 'the celebration of the memorial of the Lord's Supper' (para. 22). These sacred actions, and the ministries by which they are carried out, are clearly to be found in the Church of England. Catholic teaching is, then, that the liturgical or sacred actions of those in the Church of England 'most certainly can truly engender a life of grace and one must say, can aptly give access to the communion of salvation' (para. 3). No one who is considering full communion with the Catholic Church is, therefore, expected to deny the value of the liturgical life they have celebrated in the Church of England and, which has sustained them to this point . . .

To some, these words may seem grudging, but those who remember the apologetic invective of the past should find, as do I, ground for hope that these last months have seen progress towards that convergence for which I have tried to work in these last years and for which I still profoundly pray.

DAVID SHEPPARD: *At the heart of the common life in Churches Together in England and the Council of Churches for Britain and Ireland is the fact that we treat each other as Churches.*

Treating one another as Churches involves other Christian Churches as well as the two to which we belong. At the 1988 Lambeth Conference, Elizabeth Templeton, Church of Scotland theologian, addressed the world-wide company of Anglican bishops:

> *I rather hope the Episcopal Churches will not take off with the collective consciousness of a clump of front runners, leaving what you perceive as a handicapped assortment of Methodists, Baptists, Presbyterians, Quakers and others hobbling around the back straight! I too celebrate the immense advances made in these rich bilateral encounters between Anglicans and other Episcopal churches. But I hope that it might be your particular gift, after four centuries of 'Reformed Catholicity', to bear into the heart of these encounters the significant absence of the non-Episcopal Churches, and to interpret it.*

I have tried to bear that awareness of non-episcopal churches into all the discussions about Christian unity in which I have taken part. The unity we seek is with all the Trinitarian Churches who will come. One of our joint journeys took us to Maynooth in Ireland, to the John Paul II Society. I spoke about the effect Anglican ordination of women might have on Church Unity. I made the point that Rome was not interested simply in Anglicans: she is in conversations with Lutheran, Reformed, Methodist and Baptist Churches – all of whom have ordained women – and is concerned to find ways forward to unity with all of them. At the end of the meeting a woman came over to me and said, 'I'm so glad you said that. I'm a Lutheran priest studying here at Maynooth.'

It has been at the express request of many that we have dealt with this issue at length, precisely because some have felt dispirited over what they have themselves experienced or read. It cannot be a fully comprehensive treatment of something of which the lasting importance can only be judged in the future. We have already made it clear how important is the presence of John Newton alongside us. What has been described as 'The Mersey Miracle' is not confined to our two Churches.

Just as we asked John earlier to join us in saying what ecumenism has meant to him, so we now ask him to let us have his views and hopes for the future.

JOHN NEWTON: One of the landmarks in my own ecumenical pilgrimage was the World Council of Churches Faith and Order Conference of 1963. It was held in Montreal, and the French–Canadian Archbishop of the city, Cardinal Leger, addressed one of the sessions.

His words were both realistic and hopeful, and his ecumenical stance is one I would myself endorse. As Christians, we are already one, he claimed, by virtue of our common baptism. But we are not yet fully one, because we cannot break the one bread together. So we must press on in our pilgrimage until we can, in truth and love, share the Eucharist.

I share that vision, a vision of Christians visibly united in the one Body, where, in the words of Charles Wesley,

> *Names, and sects, and parties fall*
> *Thou, O Christ, art all in all.*

I realise that we have a long way yet to go; but we have already made great strides towards unity, and I believe that God who calls us to be one, is faithful to his promise.

That said, I must add that I do not look for a monochrome, highly regimented institution. I believe that, in any closer union of Christians, there must be, in Cardinal Hume's phrase, 'a legitimate diversity'. God's wisdom, as St Paul insists, is variegated, many-coloured, and that quality must be reflected in the life of his Church.

For my final hope for ecumenism, I return to Cardinal Leger. When he retired from his archbishopric, he spent much of the rest of his life working in a Christian mission in Africa, ministering to people afflicted with leprosy. It was mission alongside the poor. It was consonant with John Wesley's call to go, 'not only to those who need you, but to those who need you most'.

My hope and prayer is that, as Christians draw closer together, so they will work more effectively as one in their mission and service to God's children. Our united resources are called for to minister to the needs of a broken and divided world: to bring hope to the poor, the homeless, the unemployed, those dying of AIDS, those who have lost faith or never had it.

I simply add two watchwords which have spurred me on in the ecumenical pilgrimage, when it seemed a vain quest. The Abbé Paul

Couturier speaks to me when he says: 'Never give up praying for unity; one day the miracle will happen.' I resonate also the truth of a word from Edward King, the Anglican Bishop of Lincoln (1829–1910). 'The more we can draw near to Christ and fill ourselves with His Spirit, the greater power we shall have for unity. What we want is more Christlike Christians.'

After nearly twenty years together here in Liverpool, and conscious that before long the leadership of the Churches in Merseyside must be entrusted to others, our thoughts are divided between deep gratitude for having been called to serve together such fine people during what must be regarded as testing times, and at the same time heartfelt hope for their future. David came here after twenty years' ministry in inner-city London, first among East Enders and then in South London. Derek came from Westminster and Portsmouth with a double mandate from Pope Paul VI: to help the people of the archdiocese to face up to the challenge of impending social change, and to ensure that Liverpool did not 'become another Belfast'. Others will judge us. We are thankful to have been able to share the task of witnessing to Christ in a hurt city, and to have seen the thankfulness of so many at the gradual disappearance of militant sectarianism. The resilience of the people of Liverpool in face of social, economic and political hardship we have chronicled in these pages, following the more detailed treatment of the earlier years in *Better Together*. What grounds have we now for hope in the future?

Our vision for the future begins with the hope that the people of God will not weary of the quest for the fullness of unity. The generation next to our own knows how important it has been actively to renounce suspicion and rivalry and to foster trust and partnership. But we fear that a number of those in a younger generation, including some of the clergy in their early thirties, assume too easily that close relations between the Churches are a normal part of the religious scene. Perhaps a pastoral placement could be arranged for them in Northern Ireland or in the former Yugoslavia. Sadly some of them give little evidence of understanding the hard graft needed to keep a local Churches' Covenant enlivened. There is a generation which is inclined to be dismissive of the value of structures. They prefer what they see as the alternative: 'let spontaneity rule'. We recall seeing in a New Year together a decade ago. After midnight Grace Sheppard asked Derek what his hopes for the New Year might be. He said that he wished 'that young people might see the value of making lasting commitments'. He was thinking of vows for life-long marriage, and commitment to religious vocations, to long-term training for priesthood or other callings. Today such a measure of commitment is one of our heart-felt wishes for the future of those engaged in work for Christian unity.

Ecumenism is not about finding in another Church friends whose sympathies run on lines similar to our own. It is about building bridges between Churches. It is a true work for a bishop: *pontifex* is a bridge-builder. We felt honoured when for that reason Liverpool Polytechnic (now John Moores University) made us Doctors of Technology. They wanted to note the bridge-building we did in the community, but it is not only for bishops. Individuals play vital parts as planks in the bridge, even if at times they feel trampled over. Our ultimate hope is for one unified structure in which all Christians may recognise that as a community they belong to one another. If we disagree with one another, our reaching out for unity challenges us to try to understand each other better. A few months before his death, Brian Redhead delivered the first Gerald Priestland Lecture on BBC Radio 4 in the Anglican Cathedral in Liverpool. In it he pointed out that St John did not ask Christians to agree with one another; he asked them to do something much more difficult – to love one another.

Endurance, faith, hope: that is the order of the agenda set by St Paul for the early Christians. When the need is for endurance, there is often the temptation to be discouraged because the 'one Lord, one Church, one faith' still seems far away. A pause to remember the past helps us to recognise progress, but there are still separate developments and separate structures which are an obstacle to the *koinonia*, the living communion, which we seek. We are called to be the one, holy, catholic and apostolic Church: to be a company in which all barriers of race and class are broken down. Often separate developments on a denominational basis have concealed an apartheid of social groupings, in which Christians are content to be at ease, worshipping and living in like-minded company and culture. Separate development, which is the meaning of apartheid and the reverse of unity, has meant that we inherited or developed thought, acquaintances, liturgy, even hymnody, in separation: and so grew further apart. The sharing, which is the basis of the partnership we now know, helps in the achievement of that unity which we recognise as our communion in the body of Christ, the Church. The approach, though, must be well laid. We cannot rush ahead without working away at those bridges. Otherwise separation can become opposition.

DAVID SHEPPARD: We are often questioned about allowing intercommunion. Although I realise that the question is aimed particularly at Derek, I have taken to answering first: the discipline of the Church of England is to welcome to the Lord's Table all who are full members of Christian Churches. That reflects our view of the Church that it is like one great tree, and that our Church is one major branch within it. Because we believe there is only one Church, it is fitting that we should welcome members of different branches of the Church to receive Holy Communion together.

The Roman Catholic discipline – not to allow members of other churches to receive – stems from their belief that the one Church has been altogether broken apart by the sin of disunity. To receive Holy Communion is a sign of unity already achieved, of the full communion which we still seek. Therefore they believe that Eucharistic hospitality is 'papering over the cracks'. Seeing this through Roman Catholic eyes has made me uneasy about the almost casual way in which Christians sometimes receive, without any acknowledgment of their responsibility to work towards bridge-building between the Churches.

Among my hopes for fresh planks in the bridge towards unity is that eucharistic hospitality may be allowed, where there is a clear commitment to ecumenical structures, such as a Covenant between Churches or a Local Ecumenical Project.

Sometimes people complain to us that they can make no further progress until eucharistic hospitality is extended beyond the quite exceptional circumstances where at present it seems permitted, e.g. times of persecution, or distance from an Anglican celebration for 'a long period' (however that is interpreted). Much must depend on the outcome of the difficulties, insights and opportunities of which we have written in relation to the Anglican decision to ordain women to the priesthood. Yet we know that if and when that blessed day comes – and we pray for this – the Kingdom of God will not yet have arrived. There will still be points to be resolved and truths to be upheld in face of secularism which advances apace. We shall still face many disappointments on our journey. However, we do not walk alone, but with the Risen Lord who is the source of the hope in our hearts.

True enough, as we look at increasingly secularised and materialist Britain, it is not easy to recognise grounds for optimism about the future. In spite of definite changes for the better during our years in Liverpool, we see few signs of a will in comfortable Britain to give sufficient priority to turn around the old cities. Without such a will, there is little chance that the large ranks of those at present excluded from good opportunities will come to feel that they are members of one national body. We once asked Ted Heath (now Sir Edward) what should be done for those industrial areas whose main product was no longer required. 'Fund them,' he replied bluntly. 'And what if large industrial cities have the same problem?' we continued. 'Bigger funds,' he replied succinctly. Can we hope that where there is a will, there will be available funds? Optimism about some proximate great age of progress and prosperity seems unrealistic.

As we look at young people growing up today in Liverpool, our hope is that they will find in the Church a genuine concern for the conditions in which they must find fulfilment, and a united and faithful witness to the relevance of Christ's teaching to their lives; and we pray that this will help them to see where the seeds of change and of salvation are to be found. We have in this book often quoted from the documents of the Second Vatican Council, for they recalled for us the renewal of Christian life with which we are concerned. At this point we are mindful of its reference to the Church as a 'messianic people' which, 'although it does not actually include all people, and at times may appear as a small flock, is, however, a most sure seed of unity, hope and salvation for the whole human race'. (*Lumen Gentium*, Article 9).

We have recently come across a parable which Bishop Leslie Hunter used to tell when he was Anglican Bishop of Sheffield in the years following the Second World War. As the threats of war and the cries of the dispossessed were heard, Western Humanity fell into an uneasy sleep and dreamed: the dream was of entering the spacious store in which the gifts of God to all people are kept, and of speaking to the angel behind the counter: 'I have run out of the fruits of the Spirit. Can you restock me?' When the angel seemed about to say No, there was a desperate plea. 'In place of war, afflictions, injustice, lying and lust, I need love, joy, peace, integrity, discipline. Without these I shall be lost.' And the angel behind the counter replied, 'We do not stock fruits, only seeds' (*The Seed and the Fruit*, Leslie Hunter, SCM Press, 1953).

We end as we began, in Liverpool. Our minds turn back to April 1989. The Hillsborough Memorial Service, concluding the city's two weeks of mourning, is coming to an end.

Cardinal Basil Hume comes forward to pray: God grant to the living, grace; to the departed, rest; to the Church, the Nation and the Commonwealth, unity, peace and concord, through Jesus Christ our Lord. Amen.

Archibishop John Habgood of York pronounces the blessing: Go forth into the world in peace; be of good courage; hold fast to that which is good; render to no one evil for evil; strengthen the faint-hearted, support the weak; help the afflicted; honour all people; love and serve the Lord, rejoicing in the power of the Spirit. And the blessing of God Almighty, the Father, the Son and the Holy Spirit, be upon you and remain with you always. Amen.

There is a profound silence, which at last is broken by the treble voice of a single chorister singing 'You'll never walk alone'. It has been heard on countless occasions in the previous fortnight, in cathedrals, churches, at the Anfield football pitch, wherever Liverpudlians have gathered in mutual support . . .

As first the chorister and then the choir come to the end of the chorus, all the members of the vast congregation rise to their feet and, as we do now, make the words their own:

> When you walk through a storm
> Hold your head up high
> And don't be afraid of the dark.
> At the end of the road there's a golden sky
> And the sweet silver song of a lark.
> Walk on through the wind,
> Walk on through the rain,
> Though your dreams be tossed and blown;
> Walk on, walk on *with hope in your heart*
> And you'll never walk alone,
> You'll never walk alone.

Index

Index